God's Desi[gn]

MACHINES & MOTION

1:1
answersingenesis
Petersburg, Kentucky, USA

3RD EDITION | UPDATED, EXPANDED & FULL COLOR

ANSWERS IN GENESIS **SCIENCE** BY DEBBIE & RICHARD LAWRENCE

God's Design® for the Physical World is a complete physical science curriculum for grades 3–8. The books in this series are designed for use in the Christian school and homeschool, and provide easy-to-use lessons that will encourage children to see God's hand in everything around them.

Third edition
Third printing February 2012

Copyright © 2008 by Debbie and Richard Lawrence

ISBN: 1-60092-158-2

Cover design: Brandie Lucas & Diane King
Layout: Diane King
Editors: Lori Jaworski, Gary Vaterlaus

The publisher and authors have made every reasonable effort to ensure that the activities recommended in this book are safe when performed as instructed but assume no responsibility for any damage caused or sustained while conducting the experiments and activities. It is the parents', guardians', and/or teachers' responsibility to supervise all recommended activities.

Published by Answers in Genesis, 2800 Bullittsburg Church Rd., Petersburg KY 41080

Printed in China

www.answersingenesis.org • www.godsdesignscience.com

PHOTO CREDITS

TABLE OF CONTENTS

Unit 1 - Mechanical Forces

Lesson 1   Introduction to Mechanical Energy   8

Lesson 2   Potential & Kinetic Energy   10

Lesson 3   Conservation of Energy   13

Lesson 4   Conservation of Momentum   16

Special Feature   Perpetual Motion   19

Lesson 5   Force   21

Lesson 6   Friction   24

Lesson 7   Work   26

Lesson 8   Power   29

Unit 2 - Simple Machines

Lesson 9   Simple Machines   32

Special Feature   Archimedes   34

Lesson 10   Inclined Planes   36

Lesson 11   Wedges & Screws   38

Lesson 12   Levers   41

Lesson 13   First-, Second-, & Third-Class Levers   45

Lesson 14   Wheels & Axles   48

Lesson 15   Gears   51

Lesson 16   Pulleys   54

Unit 3 - Kinematics

Lesson 17   Kinematics   58

Lesson 18   Speed & Velocity.   60

Lesson 19   Acceleration   63

Lesson 20   Theory of Relativity   66

Special Feature   Albert Einstein   69

Unit 4 - Dynamics

Lesson 21   First Law of Motion   72

Lesson 22   Second Law of Motion   75

Lesson 23   Third Law of Motion   78

Lesson 24   Gravity   80

Lesson 25   Falling Bodies   84

Lesson 26   Center of Mass   87

Unit 5 - Circular & Periodic Motion

Lesson 27   Circular Motion   91

Lesson 28   Motion of the Planets   94

Special Feature   Johannes Kepler   97

Lesson 29   Periodic Motion   99

Lesson 30   Pendulums   102

Special Feature   Christian Huygens   104

Unit 6 - Use of Machines

Lesson 31   Machines in History   106

Lesson 32   Machines in Nature   109

Lesson 33   Modern Machines.   112

Lesson 34   Using Simple Machines—Final Project   115

Lesson 35   Conclusion   117

Glossary   118

Index   121

WELCOME TO
GOD'S DESIGN®
FOR THE PHYSICAL WORLD

You are about to start an exciting series of lessons on physical science. *God's Design® for the Physical World* consists of three books: *Heat and Energy*, *Machines and Motion*, and *Inventions and Technology*. Each of these books will give you insight into how God designed and created our world and the universe in which we live.

No matter what grade you are in, third through eighth grade, you can use this book.

3rd–5th grade

Read the lesson and then do the activity in the ▬▬ box (the worksheets will be provided by your teacher). After you complete the activity, test your understanding by answering the questions in the ▬▬ box. Be sure to read the special features and do the final project.

6th–8th grade

Read the lesson and then do the activity in the ▬▬ box. After you complete the activity, test your understanding by answering the questions in the ▬▬ box. Also do the "Challenge" section in the ▬▬ box. This part of the lesson will challenge you to do more advanced activities and learn additional interesting information. Be sure to read the special features and do the final project.

There are also unit quizzes and a final test to take.

Throughout this book you will see special icons like the one to the right. These icons tell you how the information in the lessons fit into the Seven C's of History: Creation, Corruption, Catastrophe, Confusion, Christ, Cross, Consummation. Your teacher will explain these to you.

When you truly understand how God has designed everything in our universe to work together, then you will enjoy the world around you even more. So let's get started!

UNIT 1

MECHANICAL FORCES

KEY CONCEPTS

◊ **Distinguish** between kinetic and potential energy.

◊ **Describe** how energy and matter are related to one another.

◊ **Explain** how momentum is conserved in collisions.

◊ **Describe** how force, work, power, and friction are related.

UNIT LESSONS

1 **Introduction to Mechanical Energy • 8**

2 **Potential & Kinetic Energy • 10**

3 **Conservation of Energy • 13**

4 **Conservation of Momentum • 16**

5 **Force • 21**

6 **Friction • 24**

7 **Work • 26**

8 **Power • 29**

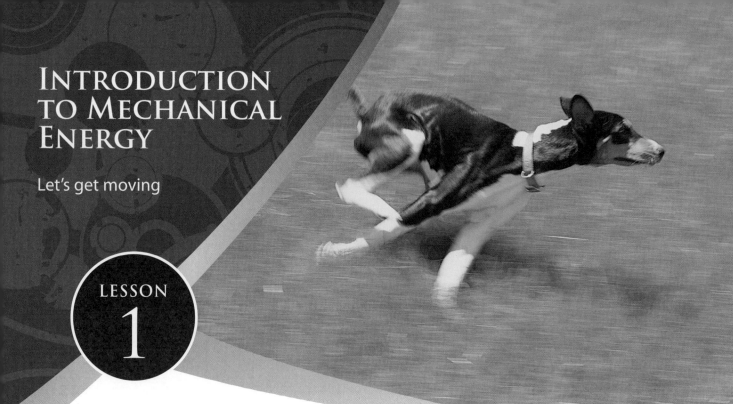

INTRODUCTION TO MECHANICAL ENERGY

Let's get moving

LESSON 1

What is mechanical energy?

Words to know:

mechanics

mechanical energy

energy

Challenge words:

physical laws

Sit very, very still. Try not to move at all. Try to imagine what the world would be like if nothing moved. It would be a very boring place. Thankfully, God loves motion and created a universe full of movement. There are certainly times to be still. Psalm 46:10 says, "Be still, and know that I am God." However, the world around us is in constant motion.

The scientific study of motion is called **mechanics**, or the study of mechanical energy. In this book, you will learn about the different ways things move, why they move, and many ways to use that motion. Motion can be in a straight line or in an arc. If something is moving around an axis, it is said to have circular motion. Gravity plays a large role in how things move on earth. So we will be studying about gravity in this book.

Mechanical energy is one of the most visible types of energy. Other types of energy include chemical, electrical, light, nuclear, and thermal (heat). Unlike chemical, nuclear, and electrical energy, which all take place on a microscopic and atomic level, mechanical energy is easily seen, measured, and tested. You see things and people move all around you.

Like all forms of **energy**, from a scientific viewpoint mechanical energy is the ability to perform work. You perform work when you move something. You use mechanical energy in countless ways. You use it to brush your teeth and comb your hair. You use mechanical energy to ride a bike or mow the lawn. Mechanical energy swings a bat to hit a home run and allows you to slide down a snowy hill.

People have also learned to build machines that allow them to do much more work than they could without the machines. Using a machine to increase your ability to do work is called mechanical advantage. Mechanical advantage allows people to build bridges, skyscrapers, aircraft carriers, and airplanes. You will enjoy your study of mechanics—so let's get moving. ■

EXPERIMENTING WITH MOTION

Let's examine the different ways that objects move. Complete the activities described on the "Types of Motion" worksheet. Record your observations and answer the questions as you do them.

WHAT DID WE LEARN?

- What is mechanics?
- What is energy?
- What are some ways that objects move?

TAKING IT FURTHER

- What force greatly affects motion on earth?
- List three or more ways that mechanical advantage is being used around you.

PHYSICAL LAWS

All objects in the universe move according to specific laws. For example, all objects obey the law of gravity. Everything on earth is pulled toward the center of the earth. We will be studying many of the scientific or physical laws that govern movements of objects.

These physical laws are different from other types of laws.

1. Physical laws were not invented by men—they are only described by men.
2. Physical laws cannot be broken or changed.
3. Physical laws apply throughout the entire universe.
4. Physical laws were set in place by God.

Based on your observations throughout your life, write down what physical laws you think apply to moving objects.

POTENTIAL & KINETIC ENERGY

Ready to move

LESSON 2

How do potential and kinetic energy differ?

Words to know:

kinetic energy

potential energy

Energy can exist in one of two forms. Either it is being used or it is being stored. Energy that is being used is called **kinetic energy**. Energy that is being stored is called **potential energy**.

Mechanical energy is the energy of motion. Mechanical energy is being used if an object is moving. A moving object has kinetic energy. If an object is not moving, but has the ability to move, it has potential energy. For example, a rock at the top of a hill may not be moving, but it has the ability to roll down the hill so it has potential energy.

Potential energy is stored energy. It is related to an object's position or condition. In the previous example, the rock has potential energy because of its position at the top of the hill. Objects that are above ground level have potential energy because gravity is pulling down on them and giving them the potential to move downward—this is called gravitational potential energy.

Other objects have potential energy because of their condition. A stretched spring has potential energy because it is stretched beyond its natural resting position. Similarly, a compressed spring also has potential energy. In either case, if the force holding the spring is released, the spring

These boulders have potential energy.

CONVERSION OF ENERGY

Hold a book a few inches above the table and drop it. Describe the conversion of energy that just occurred.

Purpose: To have fun with potential energy by making and playing a rubber band target game

Materials: paper or cardboard, drawing compass, pencil, markers, rubber bands

Procedure:

1. Use a compass to draw a target with several circles inside each other. If you don't have a compass, trace around several different sized round objects.

2. Label the circles with point numbers. For example, place a 100 inside the smallest circle. The next circle could be worth 50 points, the next largest circle could be 25 points, and so on.

3. Place the target across the room and take turns shooting rubber bands at the target.

4. Keep track of who gets the highest score.

Describe the conversion of energy that is occurring as you shoot a rubber band.

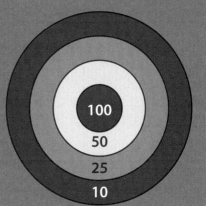

will move back to its natural position, thus converting the potential energy into kinetic energy.

As you can see from the spring example, potential energy can be easily converted into kinetic energy. Another example of this conversion is a swinging pendulum. At the top of its swing, a pendulum is not moving so all it has is potential energy. During the swing, the pendulum has some potential and some kinetic energy. At the bottom of the swing, all the potential energy has been converted into kinetic energy. Once the pendulum begins to move upward, the kinetic energy begins to be converted into potential energy again. ■

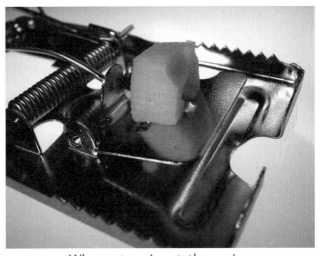

When a trap is set, the spring has potential energy.

WHAT DID WE LEARN?

- What is potential energy?
- What is kinetic energy?
- Give several examples of objects with potential energy.
- Give several examples of objects with kinetic energy.

TAKING IT FURTHER

- Describe the transfer of energy between kinetic and potential energy that occurs during a roller coaster ride.
- Explain how a wind-up clock uses potential and mechanical energy.

CALCULATING ENERGY

The amount of potential energy contained in an object can be calculated if you know the object's mass and its height above the surface to which it would fall. The gravitational potential energy of an object is equal to its mass times its height times the acceleration due to gravity. This relationship is expressed in the equation, $U = mgh$, where U represent potential energy (in joules), m is mass (in kilograms; note: 1 kg = 2.2 pounds), g is acceleration due to gravity (in meters/second^2), and h is height (in meters). The acceleration due to gravity is the same for all objects on earth and is equal to 9.8 meters/second^2.

This book has a mass of approximately 0.4 kilograms. Hold it above the table and measure its height. Now use the equation above to calculate its potential energy. How is the potential energy changed if you hold the book above the floor instead of above the table?

Kinetic energy can be calculated by the equation, $K = \frac{1}{2}mv^2$. Like potential energy, kinetic energy is measured in joules and in this equation, m is mass in kilograms and v is velocity in meters per second. If you throw a 2-kilogram softball at a velocity of 5 meters per second, what will its kinetic energy

be? What will its kinetic energy be if you throw it at 10 m/s?

Kinetic energy increases four times when the velocity is doubled because it is a function of velocity squared. How would the stopping distance required for a car traveling at 40 kilometers per hour compare to the stopping distance of a car traveling at 80 km/h?

To gain some practice using these equations, complete the "Calculating Energy" worksheet. For a fun project, design a boat, car, or other object that uses the potential energy stored in a stretched rubber band as its power source.

FUN FACT

Potential energy does not just refer to mechanical energy. Other forms of energy can be stored as well. Some other forms of potential energy include:
- A charged battery
- Chemical bonds
- Atomic bonds

These forms of potential energy are then changed into kinetic energy.
- The flow of electricity
- Breaking of chemical bonds can release heat
- Breaking of atomic bonds releases huge amounts of heat and light

CONSERVATION OF ENERGY

Can it be used up?

How are mass and energy related?

Words to know:

law of conservation of energy

law of conservation of mass

first law of thermodynamics

As you learned in the previous lesson, potential energy is easily converted into kinetic energy, and kinetic energy is easily converted into potential energy. We see examples of this energy conversion all around us, from elevators and escalators to clocks and scales. Not only does potential energy get converted into kinetic energy, but different forms of energy are converted into other forms. For example, when you eat food you are adding chemical energy to your body. That chemical energy is converted into heat and mechanical energy. When you use a telephone, the sound energy in your voice is converted into electricity on your end and the electricity is converted back into sound energy on the other end of the call.

Scientists have studied the changing forms of energy for hundreds of years and have discovered that although energy frequently changes form, it does not get used up. This is called conservation of energy. Conservation of energy is a very important concept. If even a little bit of energy were used up every time energy changed form, in a short period of time all of the energy would be gone and this world would cease to exist. However, God designed the world so that energy is conserved.

The definition of the **law of conservation of energy** states that energy cannot be created or destroyed; it can only change form. This leads to a very important question. If energy cannot be created by any known natural processes, where did all the energy around us come from? There are various ideas about how the universe came to be the way it is. Many evolutionists claim that the stars and planets were formed through a process that took billions of years. But none of the evolutionary ideas can explain where the energy came from to

ENERGY TRANSFORMATIONS

Complete the "Energy Conservation" worksheet, and then discuss the answers.

Mechanical Forces

begin with. On the other hand, the Bible explains that God spoke the universe into existence. He put all of the energy into the universe to begin with, and then designed it so that the energy could not be destroyed.

Albert Einstein and other scientists discovered that there is a close relationship between mass and energy. This relationship is expressed in the famous equation $E=mc^2$, where E is energy, m is mass, and c is the speed of light. This means that all mass has energy, and all energy has mass. Mass and energy are each conserved in any reaction. The **first law of thermodynamics** is a generalized form of the law of conservation of energy. It states that in a closed system, energy can neither be created nor destroyed, only transformed or transferred. In other words, energy is conserved.

Scientists have discovered a similar law relating to mass. When chemical reactions take place, the atoms are rearranged, but no atoms are destroyed or lost. None of the mass is lost in these reactions. The **law of conservation of mass** states that matter cannot be created or destroyed; it can only change forms.

God created all matter and energy, and then set physical laws in place so that the universe is the ultimate recycling machine. ∎

WHAT DID WE LEARN?

- What is the law of conservation of energy?

- What is the first law of thermodynamics?

- What is the law of conservation of mass?

- What happens to mechanical energy that causes a moving object to slow down and eventually stop?

TAKING IT FURTHER

- If we lived in a world with no friction, what would happen to a toy car when you pushed it across the floor?

- What famous equation did Einstein publish that explains how mass and energy are related?

- Based on your observations, what is the most likely final form of energy?

14 · MACHINES & MOTION   LESSON 3

Electrical energy is the most versatile form of energy. It can easily be converted into most other forms of energy. What forms of energy is electricity being converted into in your house? Other forms of energy are not as useful. Heat from friction is considered waste heat because it cannot easily be captured and turned into any other form of energy. Similarly, most sound and light energy eventually become heat and cannot be reused. So although the energy still exists, it may not exist in a useful form.

JOULE'S EXPERIMENT

James Joule was the first scientist to show that heat is a form of energy that can be converted from mechanical energy. Joule's experiment of the 1840s consisted of a brass paddle wheel stirring water in a copper vessel. The paddle wheel was turned by falling weights. As the paddle wheel turned, the temperature of the water rose by an amount that depended on how far the weights fell. Different weights produced different changes in temperature. Joule showed a direct relationship between the mechanical force of each weight and the change in the temperature of the water. Energy was conserved in this experiment.

Explain how the movement of the paddles increases the temperature of the water.

For an exciting biography on this great Christian scientist, see www.answersingenesis.org/go/joule.

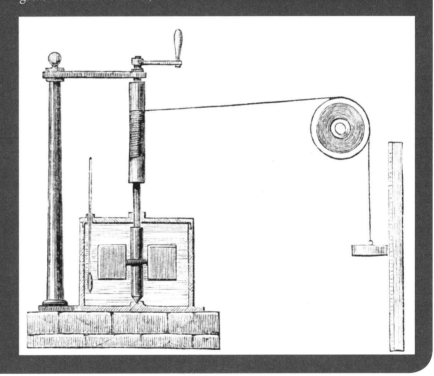

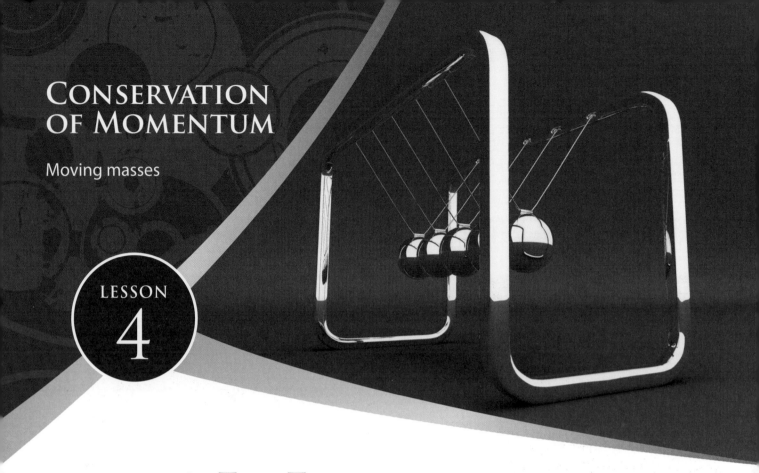

CONSERVATION OF MOMENTUM

Moving masses

LESSON 4

What is momentum?

Words to know:

momentum

law of conservation of momentum

Moving objects are said to have momentum. Momentum is a function of an object's mass and its velocity. Because velocity is speed in a particular direction, **momentum** is movement in a particular direction. If two objects have the same mass and are moving in the same direction, the object with the greater velocity will have the greater momentum. As an object's velocity increases, so does its momentum.

Similarly, if two objects are traveling at the same velocity, the object with the greater mass will have the greater momentum. For example, if a small car and a tractor-trailer are both traveling down the highway at 60 mph (97 km/h), the truck will have significantly more momentum than the car because it has more mass. This is why a tractor-trailer requires a much longer stopping distance than a small car.

In a given isolated system, momentum must be conserved. This means that if two objects are traveling toward each other and collide, the total momentum after the collision must be the same as the total momentum before the collision. We observe this happening all around us but may not recognize this as a law of physics. Consider the batter in a baseball game. As he swings the bat, it has a certain mass and velocity so it has momentum. The pitcher pitches the ball. As the ball is moving toward the batter, it has mass and velocity so it also has momentum. As the ball connects with the bat, most of the momentum from the bat is transferred to the ball, causing it to change direction and increase in velocity. The rest of the bat's momentum carries it through the completion of the swing. The **law of conservation of momentum** states that changes of momentum in an isolated system must be equal. Therefore, if the momentum of the bat and the ball were added up just prior

OBSERVING MOMENTUM

Purpose: To observe the effects of momentum in several different ways

Materials: six marbles, hardbound book, dominoes, ping-pong ball, golf ball

Procedure:

1. Place 4 marbles that are the same size on the edge of a hardbound book, so that they are all touching each other (see illustration).

2. Roll a fifth marble along the edge of the book. What happened when the moving marble collided with the still marbles? Why did this happen?

3. What would you expect to see happen if you rolled two marbles together toward the stationary marbles? Try this and see what happens.

4. Set up a row of dominoes in a way that if the first one falls, they will all fall in turn. Predict what will happen if you roll a ping-pong ball toward the first domino.

5. Gently roll the ball toward the dominoes. What did you observe? What do you think will happen if you roll a golf ball toward the dominoes instead? Try it and see.

Questions:

- Why was the ping-pong ball unable to knock over the dominoes?

- Why was the golf ball able to knock over the dominoes?

to the hit and just after the hit, they would have to be equal. After the hit, the ball has more momentum and the bat has less, but the total amount is the same. The amount of momentum gained by the ball is equal to the amount of momentum lost by the bat.

Because momentum is a function of mass and velocity, if a heavier object hits a lighter object, the lighter object will be accelerated more than the heavier object

WHAT DID WE LEARN?

- What is momentum?
- What two quantities affect an object's momentum?
- What is the law of conservation of momentum?

TAKING IT FURTHER

- If a large football player and a small soccer player are running toward each other, what is likely to happen to the speed and direction of each player when they collide?

- What will happen if you shoot a penny across a smooth table into a stationary penny?

- How might a ping-pong ball be made to knock over a heavy domino?

- If a golf ball is rolled very slowly, will it still knock over the dominoes?

Mechanical Forces

decelerates. The baseball bat has more mass than the ball, so it causes the ball to change directions and accelerate. If you have ever played marbles, you probably know that the shooter is larger than the other marbles so that its momentum can cause the smaller marbles to accelerate and move out of the circle. Another example is when two people jump on a trampoline together. If one person is significantly heavier than the other, the bounce from the heavier person will cause the smaller person to shoot into the air at a much faster speed.

These are all examples of transfer of momentum. And in each case, the total momentum of the objects after the collision is the same as the total momentum before. If you add up the momentum of the people before they hit the trampoline and again after they bounce, you will find that the total momentum did not change. ■

CALCULATING MOMENTUM

Momentum is described mathematically as $p = mv$, where p is the momentum, m is mass, and v is velocity. A car with a mass of 1,000 kilograms, traveling east at 50 km/h would have an eastward momentum of 50,000 kg-km/h. There are no special units for momentum—it is described in units of mass and velocity. Use the momentum equation to calculate the momentum for each of the following objects.

Object 1: A 50 kg boy running 4 meters/second in a race.

Object 2: A 45 kg girl running 4 m/s in the same race.

Who has more momentum, the boy or the girl?

Object 3: A 5 kg bowling ball rolling down the lane at 8 m/s.

Object 4: A 0.05 kg bullet flying through the air at 1,000 m/s.

How does the momentum of the bullet compare to that of the bowling ball?

Purpose: To make a Newton's Cradle and observe the conservation of momentum

Materials: five large and five small glass or heavy plastic beads, ruler, two pencils, knife, thread, four cans

Procedure:

1. Use a ruler to measure the diameter of five large beads.

2. Make five equally-spaced marks on two pencils. The marks should be the same distance apart as the diameter of the large beads.

3. Using a small knife, carefully cut a notch at each mark.

4. Cut five pieces of thread each 9 inches long and put one end through a small bead. Adjust the bead so that it is in the

center of the thread. Then push both ends of the thread through a large bead. Tie the thread at the top of the large bead to hold the beads together. (See illustration.)

5. Tie each end of the thread to one of the notches in each pencil and suspend each pencil between two cans as shown.

Now you can play with your "cradle." Draw the end bead back a short distance and let it go. What happens when it hits the other beads? Try drawing two beads back at the same time? What happens when you pull back three beads? How does this demonstrate conservation of momentum?

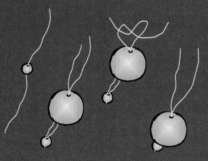

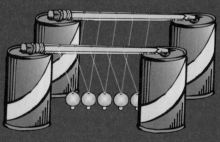

Perpetual Motion

"NIHIL EX NIHILO: NOTHING WILL PRODUCE NOTHING"

For centuries people have sought to build a perpetual motion machine—a machine which, once started, would continue to run forever. The hope was that if a wheel could be made to turn without adding energy, that motion could be used for other purposes such as grinding grain. But is a perpetual motion machine possible? Can we get something from nothing? For about the last 700 years, many men have believed this to be true; they believed we could get energy from nothing. Let's look at a couple of examples.

The earliest known drawings of a perpetual motion machine came from Villard de Honnecort whose professional career lasted between 1225 and 1250. The design was a wheel with several hammers hanging around the outside of the wheel, called an "overbalanced wheel" (see diagram above). The idea was that as a hammer fell, it would give the wheel enough energy to rotate far enough for the next hammer to fall, thus the wheel would perpetually spin. There is no evidence that he ever built this wheel, but many other people have tried this method without success.

Leonardo da Vinci studied several versions of the overbalanced wheel and showed in his writings why they would not work. He is quoted as saying, "Oh, ye seekers after perpetual motion, how many vain chimeras have you pursued? Go and take your place with the

alchemists." [A *chimera* is a mythological monster with the head of a lion, the body of a goat, and the tail of a serpent. *Alchemists* are people who sought to turn lead into gold]. He obviously did not consider designers of perpetual motion machines to be real scientists.

Between 1712 and 1719, Johann Ernst Bassler, a clock maker, studied and experimented with hundreds of perpetual motion designs. He then claimed to have come up with his own design that supposedly worked. Four of his designs were publicly demonstrated and many people saw them. In 1717 he built his largest machine and gave permission to test it. The machine was put into a room on November 12, 1717. Once it was started, the room was sealed for two weeks. When the door was opened two weeks later, the machine was still running. The door was sealed again and not opened until January 4, 1718, fifty-three days after the first time the door was sealed. The witnesses said the machine was running at about the same speed.

It was natural that he was suspected of being a fraud in this matter. One of the stories that floated around was that he had a servant in the next room turning a crank to keep the wheel in motion. To eliminate this claim, Bassler set up the machine in the middle of a large room. Others suspected that springs were hidden inside the wheel or a large shaft to keep it going. No one knows exactly how this machine worked because he only allowed a few people to look inside, and they could only see part of the machine. Also, they had to sign papers saying they would not tell what they saw. Bassler died without letting anyone know how the machines worked, and at the time of his death, he had destroyed all the working machines, so no one can prove or disprove his claims.

Still today, some people hope to make a perpetual motion machine, to get something from nothing. But no design has been shown to work. The major problem with perpetual motion machines is that some of the energy is constantly being lost due to friction. For example, as the overbalanced wheel (shown on the previous page) turns, some energy is turned into heat where the wheel turns on the axle and some energy is turned into heat due to collision with air molecules. In the diagram below, some energy is lost due to the friction between the water and the screw, and between the water and the chute and bowls. Also, there is friction between the wheel and axle, and all moving parts are colliding with air molecules.

God designed the universe with His laws in place. Energy and momentum are always conserved, so if some energy is turned into heat due to friction, the machine must eventually stop moving. Even if we could find a way to eliminate all friction, the energy could not be used for another purpose without slowing down the wheel. If energy could be made from nothing then the universe itself could run out of control. God designed a universe that is balanced and takes care of itself, and God put all the energy into it that we will need.

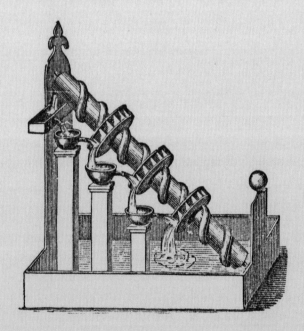

This idea shows up in many different places. The waterwheel turns the pump that pumps the water up the pipe. The water then falls into a trench and flows back to the waterwheel, turning it and pumping more water back up the pipe.

FORCE

Tug of war

LESSON 5

What is a force and how do we measure it?

Words to know:

force

tension

tensile strength

buoyancy

net force

Challenge words:

Hooke's law

We have been discussing moving objects such as a car or a person running in a race. But we have not yet discovered what makes things move. An object's motion changes because of a force that is applied to it. A force is defined as a push or a pull. Can you think of any examples of a push type of force? You push the grocery cart or a baby stroller. You also push down on your bike pedals when you ride a bike. Can you think of a pull type of force? You pull on a door to open it, and you pull out a drawer. These types of forces are mechanical forces and they affect our lives every day.

Other forces also exist. Gravity is a force that pulls down on everything on earth. We will examine gravity more in a later lesson. Electricity and magnetism also exert forces on objects. Electricity exerts force on electrons. And magnetism exerts force on magnetic materials such as iron and steel. However, in this book we will primarily be studying the mechanical forces that make objects move.

Some forces, like pushing a stroller, are easily seen. Other forces, however, are less visible. For example, consider a suspension bridge like the one shown above. The large cables are stretched very tightly to hold up the bridge. This force is a pulling force called tension. This force is constantly there, keeping the cables tight. However, if the tension were suddenly released, we would instantly see the effects of the loss of force as the cable fell down.

Different materials are able to withstand different amounts of tension. If you pulled on both ends of a piece of sewing thread, it is likely that you could snap the thread. However, if you pulled on both ends of a thick rope, it is unlikely that you could break the rope. The amount of tension that a

TESTING FORCES

Purpose: To test the tensile strength of various materials

Materials: sewing thread, two pencils, kite string, rope

Procedure:

1. Cut a piece of sewing thread at least 12 inches long.

2. Tie each end of the thread to a pencil.

3. Grasp one pencil in each hand and pull them apart until the thread breaks. How difficult was this to do?

4. Replace the sewing thread with kite string.

5. Try pulling the pencils apart until the string breaks. Were you able to break the string?

6. You will not need to tie the rope to a pencil, but you will need a partner to help you pull on a piece of rope. If you and your partner pull as hard as you can, do you break the piece of rope?

Conclusion: The rope has a much higher tensile strength than the other materials you tested and can withstand much higher tension.

Testing buoyancy: You can test buoyancy by shaping modeling clay into various shapes. Which shapes will float? Which shapes will sink? Why do some shapes sink and others float?

material can withstand is called its tensile strength. The tensile strength of a steel cable is much higher than the tensile strength of a cloth rope. Structural engineers must understand the tensile strength of various materials when designing bridges and other structures.

Another special type of mechanical force is called buoyancy. Buoyancy is a force that is exerted by liquids and gases. The force exerted by water is equal to the weight of the water that is displaced. A boat can float because it displaces enough water to cause enough force to push up on the boat to keep it from sinking. The heavier the boat, the more water it must displace in order to float.

Most objects do not experience only one force at a time. Most objects experience several forces. For example, when you throw a ball in the air, the ball experiences a push from your hand (while it is in contact with your hand) as well as a pull from the gravity of the earth. The sum of all the forces on an object is called the net force. A ball initially accelerates upward from the force of your throw, but it is constantly slowing down because of the pull of gravity. At the top of its flight, it stops moving as it changes direction. However, the force of gravity continues to pull down, so the ball begins to accelerate downward until it hits the ground where it again experiences a change of direction as the ground pushes up, and then it begins to go up again. ■

FUN FACT

It is believed that the concept of buoyancy was first understood by Archimedes while he was bathing at a public bath. He reasoned that the weight of the water displaced by his body was equal to the force of the water on his body. This principle is called the Archimedes principle in his honor. Tradition has it that Archimedes jumped from the bath and ran down the street crying, "Eureka!" (See page 34 for more on Archimedes.)

WHAT DID WE LEARN?

- What is mechanical force?
- What is tension?
- What is tensile strength?
- What is buoyancy?

TAKING IT FURTHER

- What are some of the forces that are being exerted during a basketball game?
- Why can you float more easily in the ocean than you can in a fresh water swimming pool?
- What would happen to a boat that was moving upstream at the same speed as the current was moving downstream?
- What are the forces exerted on and by a skier moving downhill?

MORE FORCES

Mechanical forces can be measured using a spring scale. The units for these measurements are called newtons in honor of Sir Isaac Newton who was considered to be one of the greatest physicists of all time. A spring stretches or compresses a certain length that is proportional to the force or weight that is applied. This is called Hooke's law and is what allows us to calibrate and use a spring scale. The amount the spring moves depends on the material that the spring is made from, but it is always proportional to the force exerted.

Although your bathroom scale is probably calibrated in pounds instead of newtons, it can still be used to measure the amount of force that is being exerted because it has a spring inside it that compresses when a force is applied to it.

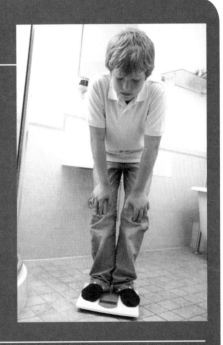

Purpose: To measure the amount of force exerted by various objects

Materials: bathroom scale

Procedure:

1. Use your hand to push on the scale as hard as you can.

2. Stand on the scale and see the effect of gravity pulling down on your body.

3. Put a book on the scale and see the effect of gravity pulling down on it.

Conclusion: Which item compressed the spring the most? This is the item that weighed the most.

Net force is the sum of all the forces acting on an object. If forces are acting in the same direction, they are added together. If forces are acting in the opposite direction, they are subtracted from each other.

Now complete the "Sum of Forces" worksheet.

FRICTION

Opposing movement

LESSON 6

What is friction and why is it important?

Words to know:

friction

lubricant

We all know that if you are roller blading or skateboarding on a flat surface you have to keep pushing if you don't want to stop moving. Why do you slow down and stop? It is because a force is acting against the movement of your wheels. This force is called **friction**. Friction is defined as a force that resists movement. Friction results from the rubbing of two objects. Try rubbing your hands together very quickly. They become warm because of the friction between the skin of your hands.

Friction is an important force all around us. It can be useful and it can be harmful. Think about how difficult it would be to walk if your feet had no friction with the ground. Your feet would slip out from under you and you would not be able to go where you want to go. You may have experienced this when you stepped onto an icy sidewalk and suddenly slipped. Similarly, friction between a car's brakes and its wheels is absolutely necessary for stopping the vehicle. Also, friction between the car's tires and the road allows the driver to have control over where the car goes. Friction is helpful in many other situations as well.

However, friction generally changes mechanical energy into heat energy and too much heat can have very damaging effects. In a car's engine, the moving parts can generate a great amount of heat. They can generate so much heat, in fact, that the metal parts can begin to melt. This can cause severe damage to the engine. Therefore, the amount of friction inside an engine must be minimized. This can be done by covering the engine parts with a substance that does not resist movement or has less friction. One type of substance used for this purpose is oil. Oil has a special molecular structure that allows the molecules to easily move over one another. That is why oil feels so slippery. Substances that reduce friction are called **lubricants**. It is vitally important that your car engine have

MEASURING FRICTION

Complete the "Friction" worksheet. Save the block of wood with the hook in it. You will be using it in several other lessons.

enough oil to keep all of the moving parts lubricated to prevent too much heat from being generated. Even with lubricants, some friction still exists and produces heat. This is why cars usually have radiators to help transfer heat away from the engine.

Because there are frictional forces between nearly all objects, in order for an object to move it is necessary to overcome those frictional forces. A wagon will not roll until enough force is added to overcome the wagon's inertia as well as to overcome the friction between the wheels and the ground and the wheels and their axles. (Inertia is an object's tendency to stay in its present condition—we will learn more about this in lesson 21.) Air molecules are constantly pushing against moving objects so energy is needed to overcome this frictional force as well. Engineers who design cars, airplanes, and other vehicles are very careful to design them so that the air molecules will have a minimal impact—to make them aerodynamic. This improves the fuel efficiency of the vehicle. The shape of the vehicle is one of the primary factors in how much air resistance will affect the motion of the vehicle. Rounded surfaces allow the air to flow more easily than flat or square surfaces. Also, smooth surfaces allow air to flow more easily than bumpy or uneven surfaces. A great deal of thought is put into how friction will affect vehicles. And although you may not think about it, friction affects every movement you make. ■

WHAT DID WE LEARN?

- What is friction?
- What is the cause of friction?
- How can friction be useful?
- How can friction be damaging?

TAKING IT FURTHER

- When would street maintenance people try to increase friction on the streets?
- How do they try to increase the friction?
- Why do drag racers use very wide treadless tires in a race?

REDUCING FRICTION

Design a way to reduce the friction between the block of wood and the various surfaces over which you pulled it.

WORK

Everyone has to do it

What is work and how do we measure it?

Words to know:

work

What do you think of when you hear the word *work*? Do you think about your dad's job? Maybe you think about the chores you do around the house or maybe you think about your school work. These are all tasks that many people consider to be work. However, from a scientific point of view work has a different meaning. The scientific definition of **work** is a change in position due to an applied force.

Recall that a force is a push or a pull. So in order for work to be done a push or a pull must make an object move. Work is described mathematically as force times distance. Let's look at the work done when you pick up your soccer ball. If you pick it up off the floor and set in on a table you do some work. If you pick it up and set it on the top shelf of your closet you do more work. The force needed to lift the ball is the same in either case because you are lifting the same ball each time, but in the second case you have lifted it a greater distance so you have done more work.

Force is directly related to mass. It takes more force to lift a heavy object than it does to lift a light object. Therefore, if you lift a volleyball from the floor to the table you will do less work than if you lift a bowling ball from the floor to the table. The distance you move each ball is the same. However, because the bowling ball has more mass, you must exert a greater force to lift it, and so you are doing more work.

The path taken to move an object does not affect

FUN FACT

The human heart is working and resting alternately 24 hours per day. The work done by your heart each day to move the blood in your body is equivalent to the work done when lifting a small car 50 feet (15 m) in the air. God designed your heart to be a mighty worker!

PERFORMING WORK

Purpose: To understand the relationship of force, distance, and work

Materials: three boxes, various items, chair

Activity 1—Procedure:

1. Place three identical boxes on the floor.

2. Put items of various weights inside the boxes so that they are all different weights.

3. Lift the first box from the floor to your waist. Think about the

force that was required to lift that box.

4. Return the first box to the floor and lift the second box to waist level. Which box required the most force to lift?

5. Return that box to the floor and lift the third box to waist level. Of the three boxes, which one required the most force to lift? Which box required you to do the most work to lift it?

Activity 2—Procedure:

1. Lift the first box and set it on a chair.

2. Place the box back on the floor.

3. Now lift the same box and place it on a kitchen counter. Which action required you to do more work?

Activity 3—Procedure:

1. Hold the first box in your arms for 1 minute. How much work are you doing to hold the box?

the amount of work done. For example, if a hiker is climbing the side of a hill, he can climb straight up the hill or he can walk back and forth across the hill going up a little at the time. Once he reaches the top he has done the same amount of work either way. The work done is equal to his weight times the height that he climbed. It probably seems harder to climb straight up the hill, but the total amount of work done is the same either way.

Also, since work requires that an object be moved, no work is done if nothing is moved, even if a force is being applied to something. Consider the bridge cables that we talked about in lesson 5. There is a constant force applied to the cables, yet nothing is moving, so no work is being done. Work was done to put the cables in place, but once they

WHAT DID WE LEARN?

- What is the scientific definition of work?
- Force is directly related to what physical property?

TAKING IT FURTHER

- Does work always have to be done in a vertical direction?
- If one student pushes very hard on a wall and a second student picks up a pencil, which student is doing the most work?
- Is there any work being done as you coast downhill on your bike?
- Is there any work being done as a space probe moves through space?

Mechanical Forces

are in place no additional work is being done. You can also think about a weight lifter. He performs work to lift the weights above his head. But once he has the bar there, he does not perform any work to keep it above his head. He has to continually apply force, but because the weights are not moving, no work is being done. You may think that it is very hard work to hold weights above your head, but according to the scientific definition of work, it doesn't take any work at all. ■

CALCULATING WORK

Work is measured in units call joules. One joule is equal to one newton-meter. The mathematical equation for work is:

W = F x D

Where *W* is work in newton-meters, *F* is force in newtons, and *D* is distance in meters.

Purpose: To calculate work

Materials: boxes from previous activity, scale, "Work Calculation" worksheet

Procedure:

2. Use a scale to measure the weight of each of the boxes in the activities on the previous page.

3. Record your measurements on the "Work Calculation" worksheet.

4. Answer the questions on the worksheet.

You can convert the weight to newtons using one of the following conversion factors:

1 pound = 4.45 newtons or

1 kilogram = 9.81 newtons

Next, measure the distance each box was lifted. Finally, calculate the work done in each case.

POWER

Getting the job done quickly

LESSON 8

What is power and how do we measure it?

Words to know:

power

How long does it take to clean your room? If you fool around and work slowly it could take a long time. If you work hard, you can accomplish a lot more in a shorter period of time. This is the idea of power. **Power** is work done over time or the rate at which work is done. Power is measured in joules per second, which are also known as watts.

If more power is applied, more work can be accomplished in a given time period, or the same amount of work can be accomplished in less time. Let's look at an example. When you walk 1,000 meters (0.6 miles) down the street you are performing work. It may take you several minutes to walk that distance. Your legs have a certain amount of power that allows you to walk at a comfortable pace. However, you could travel the same distance in a car in a much shorter period of time. The work done by the car's engine to move you 1,000 meters is the same as the work done by your body to move you that distance. However, the car's engine has much more power than your legs so it can move you at a much faster pace. The more powerful engine can perform the same amount of work in a shorter period of time.

Let's look at the example in another way. If you walked for 5 minutes you could travel a certain distance. But if you ride in a moving car for 5 minutes you will travel a much greater distance. Since your mass is the same in either case, the force to move you is the same. Therefore, the work done by the car is greater because you moved a greater distance. The car can perform more work in the same period of time than your body because it has more power.

Many machines have been invented that are much more powerful than human bodies. These machines allow humans to accomplish much more

POWER SCAVENGER HUNT

Many electrical appliances don't perform work in the way you might think. Electrical power is calculated by the number of electrons that are moved per second instead of how far an object is moved. The work done by electricity is often converted into other types of energy such as light or heat. Keep this in mind as you search for power around your house and complete the "Power Scavenger Hunt" worksheet.

work in a shorter period of time than could otherwise be accomplished. This has greatly improved our lives. Consider how much food can be grown by one farmer today with the use of modern farm equipment compared with the amount of food that was grown when a farmer could only use a horse-drawn plow. And consider how quickly that food can be transported to the people who need it. This allows people to eat more and better food, thus improving their lives. God has given people incredible creativity when it comes to using the resources He gave us to improve our lives. ■

WHAT DID WE LEARN?

- What is the scientific definition of power?
- How do machines use power to improve our lives?

TAKING IT FURTHER

- Why is a car more powerful than a bicycle?
- A car's engine does the same amount of work to move you as a passenger as your body does when you walk. However, a car engine must be able to do more work than your body as it moves. Why?

CALCULATING POWER

Complete the "Calculating Power" worksheet to calculate how long you could run each item if you had 10,000 joules of energy. Recall that 1 watt of power is equal to 1 joule per second. So a 100-watt light bulb will use 10,000 joules of energy in 100 seconds. You simply divide the number of joules by the number of watts to determine the number of seconds each item would run on the given amount of energy. Which item requires the least amount of energy to use? Which requires the greatest amount?

Mechanical Forces

UNIT

2

SIMPLE MACHINES

KEY CONCEPTS

◊ **Describe** how inclined planes, wedges, and screws create a mechanical advantage.

◊ **Illustrate** the three types of levers using diagrams.

◊ **Explain** how wheels and gears create a mechanical advantage.

◊ **Describe** the mechanical advantage of pulley systems.

UNIT LESSONS

 9 Simple Machines • 32
10 Inclined Planes • 36
11 Wedges & Screws • 38
12 Levers • 41
13 First, Second, & Third-Class Levers • 45
14 Wheels & Axles • 48
15 Gears • 51
16 Pulleys • 54

SIMPLE MACHINES

Working for us

LESSON 9

What are simple machines?

Words to know:

mechanical advantage

distance principle

In the previous lesson we learned that machines can be very helpful. They can apply more power so we can accomplish more work in a given period of time. But before we can understand the workings of something as complicated as a car or even a hair dryer, it is a good idea to learn about the simple machines that have been used to build these complex machines.

Machines and tools help us use less force to accomplish a task. Sir Isaac Newton and other scientists have discovered that there is a link between force, work, and distance. If the work can be done over a greater distance, then less force is needed at any one time to accomplish the same amount of work. Recall our example of the hiker climbing a hill. We said that the same amount of work is done whether the hiker climbs straight up the hill or whether he zigzags back and forth as he climbs upward. This is true. However, if you have ever climbed a hill, you know that it seems much easier to zigzag. This is because it takes less force with each step if you go up the hill over a longer distance. The work has been spread out over a longer distance so less force is needed at any one time. This is the idea behind the simple machines that we will study.

There are two basic machines that are used to reduce force and increase distance so that work is easier to accomplish. The first is the one used in the hiking example. Although the hiker is going back and forth, he is basically using the side of the mountain as a ramp

MECHANICAL ADVANTAGE

Machines have been invented to make people's jobs easier. They help us achieve mechanical advantage so we can accomplish work that we would not be able to do otherwise. Look at several machines around your house. Try to identify the use of levers and inclined planes. Many of these simple machines have been modified and may not look like you expect. Inclined planes have been modified and used as screws, knives, and other blades. Levers have been modified and are used as wheels, pulleys, and gears. See how many of these simple machines you can identify in the tools and machines in your home.

Simple Machines

or inclined plane. Inclined planes are used in many ways to allow us to move objects with less force. The second simple machine is the lever. Levers are used to lift objects with less force by applying that force over a greater distance. We will examine each of these simple machines as well as several of their applications in following lessons.

The ability to move an object with less force is called **mechanical advantage**. This mechanical advantage is not "free." You must pay for the advantage by applying the force over a longer distance. This is called the **distance principle**. The hiker used less effort with each step, but walked a much greater distance in order to reach the top of the hill by zigzagging back and forth. He paid for the easier steps by taking many more of them. ■

An inclined plane makes work easier.

WHAT DID WE LEARN?

- What are the two simple machines on which all machines are based?
- Why are simple machines useful?
- What is mechanical advantage?
- How do we "pay" for mechanical advantage?

TAKING IT FURTHER

- How does the work involved in moving a piano up a ramp compare with the work needed to lift it straight up the same distance?
- When might someone choose not to use a simple machine's mechanical advantage?

MACHINE RESEARCH

Choose a machine that you would like to know more about. Research that machine and learn how it works. Draw a diagram of the basic design of the machine and write a few paragraphs explaining how it works. Be sure to include an explanation of how simple machines are used to help make the work easier.

Archimedes

287–212 BC

In the third century BC, Rome's army was a formidable force. The city-state of Syracuse had an alliance with Rome, but when its king died the city's new kings (two brothers) decided to ally themselves with Carthage, Rome's enemy. This brought the Roman army and navy against the city. Marcus Claudius Marcellus attacked the city by sea using sixty battleships called quinqueremes, while his co-commander attacked by land. The two Roman commanders felt they would have the city won in five days; however, this was not to be. As the battleships entered the harbor many of them caught fire. Others were hit with large stones that caused significant damage and killed many men. As the battleships neared the city walls, long beams with hooks swung out over the water. The hooks were lowered until they got hold of a ship. Then the hooks were raised, lifting the ship partially out of the water and either overturning it or dropping it back into the water so hard that it sank.

The army that was attacking the city by land was not faring any better. As the army tried to advance, boulders weighing as much as 500 pounds were hurled from the city walls, mowing down the Roman army. The Roman army learned quickly that they could not con-quer this city in just a few days. How could the city hold off the Romans so successfully? It was because of one man, Archimedes. Who was Archimedes and how did he accomplish so much?

Archimedes is considered to be one of the top three mathematicians of all time. He determined the most accurate number for pi (π) for his day, he developed the relationship between a sphere and a cylinder, and he started the concept of integral calculus, which was later fully developed by Sir Isaac Newton. But this is not what he is best remembered for. It was the defenses he built for his city, and some of the other practical tools he built, that have brought Archimedes his greatest fame.

Archimedes was one of the greatest scientists of his day and applied what he knew to the building of many useful tools and weapons. One tool designed

Archimedes screw

by Archimedes that is still in use today is called the Archimedes screw. The screw is used to lift large amounts of water with a small amount of force. It is believed that he designed the screw while on a trip to Egypt to help irrigate the farmers' fields.

Archimedes is also credited with being the first to understand buoyancy. The king had given a goldsmith some gold to make a crown. When the goldsmith gave the crown to the king, it had the correct weight but the king suspected that some silver had been used instead of only gold. He asked Archimedes if he could find a way to test the crown. Because of the shape of the crown, Archimedes could not accurately determine the volume of the crown. Then one day when he was getting into a bath he noticed the water that went over the side. He reasoned that the amount of water that overflowed the tub was equal to the amount of his body that was submerged and this gave him the information he needed to find the size or volume of any object regardless of its shape. He was so happy he went running down the street shouting "Eureka! Eureka!" (I have found it!). Using this method, Archimedes was able to determine the volume and density of the crown and discovered that the goldsmith had indeed mixed the gold with silver.

Now you might want to know how he was able to stop the Roman army. The story started years earlier when the king, the one friendly to Rome, asked Archimedes to build the defenses for the city. Archimedes set up several lines of defense. One story says that the long-range defenses included mirrors to focus the sun's light on a small area. Using these he was able to set the battleships' sails on fire.

By setting up large, medium, and small catapults, the city was able to hurl large stones at the battleships when they first came into the harbor and to keep up the rain of stones as the battleships advanced toward the city walls.

Using the catapults and mirrors, the citizens of Syracuse were able to destroy many of the battleships. However, many ships still made it close to the city walls. Several of these ships had large ladders on them to be set up against the walls. Many soldiers were ready to rush up these ladders and take the walls. However, as the battleships neared the walls, long wooden beams swung out on top of the walls or slid out of holes along the bottom of the walls. The lower beams were used as levers to lift the battleships and tip them over. Some of the beams on top had large stones on ropes that were moved over the top of the battleships. The stones were released, causing large amounts of damage. Other beams had hooks on the ends of their ropes that were dropped onto the ships. Then, once made fast to the ship, the ropes, using a pulley system, lifted the ship up out of the water and either dropped it there or smashed it into the rocks.

The devastation to the Roman army and navy made them withdraw and set up a siege around the city. This siege lasted eight months, until one night the people inside the city were having a festival and neglected to keep the walls well manned. At this point General Marcellus saw his chance and had his army attack the city.

Once the city was taken, the Roman soldiers were allowed to pillage the city. It is not entirely clear what happened next, but the most common story is that the soldiers were told not to hurt Archimedes. But when a Roman soldier came to Archimedes' home and found him drawing diagrams in the sand, which was a common practice for him, Archimedes only said, "I beg you, don't disturb this." At this point, the soldier was so enraged that he pulled out his sword and slew Archimedes. This was a sad end for a man with a great mathematical and scientific mind. Many accounts say that when the Roman general found out about Archimedes' death, he had the soldier killed.

INCLINED PLANES

Sliding it up

LESSON 10

How do inclined planes help us do work?

Words to know:

inclined plane

One of the earliest known uses of an inclined plane was in the building of the Egyptian pyramids. Papyrus records show that one ramp was at least 420 yards (384 m) long and 35 yards (32 m) high. So we know that ramps, or **inclined planes**, have been used for thousands of years to reduce the effort needed to move objects.

An inclined plane uses the distance principle to reduce the effort needed to move an object. Consider trying to lift a heavy box of books from the floor to the table. You may or may not be able to lift the box depending on how strong you are. If the books weighed 500 newtons, you would have to exert 500 newtons of force to lift the box 1.5 meters to the top of the table. However, if you had a smooth ramp that was 6 meters long, you could set the top of the ramp on the table and push the box up the ramp with much less effort. Because you would be moving the box 6 meters instead of 1.5, you would only need one fourth as much force; you would only need to exert 125 newtons of force to move the box to the table (see diagram below).

What you saved in effort you paid for in distance. This is preferable in many instances. A road winds up the side of a steep mountain so that a car engine does not need as much power to climb the mountain. Also, buildings are

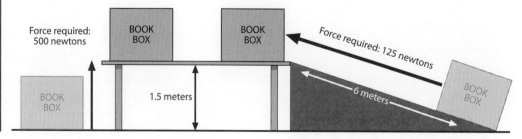

Force required: 500 newtons

BOOK BOX

BOOK BOX

BOOK BOX

1.5 meters

Force required: 125 newtons

6 meters

BOOK BOX

EXPERIMENTING WITH RAMPS

You can measure the mechanical advantage of various ramps by completing the measurements on the "Inclined Planes" worksheet.

equipped with stairs, which are a modified version of a ramp. This allows you to easily go from one floor to another. Imagine how difficult it would be if you had to pull yourself up by climbing a rope every time you needed to go upstairs. The rope would take up less room in your house, but you would have to exert more effort to go up.

Mechanical advantage is the savings in effort achieved by using the inclined plane. This can be calculated by dividing the length of the ramp by the height that the object is lifted. In our previous example, the books were lifted 1.5 meters. The ramp was 6 meters long. So the mechanical advantage was 6/1.5 = 4. This means that it was four times as easy to lift the box using the ramp than it would be to lift it straight up. If the ramp had been 7.5 meters long, it would have been 5 times as easy to push the box up the ramp. In general, the shorter and steeper the ramp, the less the mechanical advantage will be. The longer the ramp, the greater the mechanical advantage will be. ■

WHAT DID WE LEARN?

- What is an inclined plane?
- Why do people use inclined planes?
- What is mechanical advantage?
- How do you "pay" for mechanical advantage?

TAKING IT FURTHER

- What is the mechanical advantage of a ramp that is 50 meters long and has a height of 10 meters?
- List several examples of where you see ramps or inclined planes at work.

REDUCING FRICTION

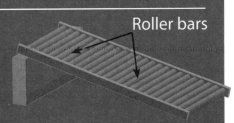

Roller bars

Ramps help to reduce the effort needed to move objects up to a different height. The efficiency of ramps is greatly affected by the amount of friction they produce. Friction between the surface of the ramp and the item being pushed increases the effort needed to lift the item. If friction can be reduced, then the effort can also be reduced.

In this book, when we calculate mechanical advantage we ignore the effects of friction; we say that the advantage is achieved with an ideal ramp—one without friction. But in the real world, we always have to deal with friction. You will be introduced to the math needed to deal with friction in a high school physics course, but for now we will look at equations without friction.

How does a ramp like this one improve efficiency?

WEDGES & SCREWS

Divide and conquer

LESSON 11

How do wedges and screws help us do work?

Words to know:

wedge

screw

bolt

pitch

Inclined planes are simple machines that make it easier to lift a weight. A ramp is a common inclined plane. However, inclined planes are used in many other forms as well. One of the most common forms is a wedge. A **wedge** is actually two inclined planes placed bottom to bottom to form a point. You may be familiar with a wedge that is used to split wood. The wedge is placed in a crack in the wood then hammered in until the wood splits. This works because the force applied to the wedge is multiplied by the mechanical advantage of the sloping sides of the wedge, allowing it to be forced into the wood more easily.

We see wedges on many tools that are used for cutting or splitting. For example, the head of an axe or a hatchet is a wedge. Also, knives, chisels, and scissors have wedges as their cutting edges. These angled edges increase the mechanical advantage so that you can use less force to cut through paper, fabric, wood, or other materials. Have you ever used a dull knife? It takes a lot more force to cut something with a dull knife than with a sharp one. When you sharpen your knife, you are restoring the edge, which allows the item you are cutting to "get on the ramp" more easily, thus allowing you to use the mechanical advantage of an inclined plane to cut the item.

A second modified form of an inclined plane that we use every day is a screw. A **screw** is an inclined plane that has been wrapped around a cylinder or cone. If the plane is wrapped around a cylinder and has a flat end it is actually called a **bolt**. A bolt with a nut screwed on the end can be used to hold two items tightly together. The mechanical advantage of the inclined plane holds the nut in place and keeps the items from coming apart.

If a plane is wrapped around a cone and comes to a point, it is called a screw.

A screw is used to force its way into a piece of wood or metal. The threads of the screw hold the object in place. The distance between the threads of a screw or bolt is called the **pitch**. The threads on the bolt shown here are much closer than the threads on the screw; therefore, it has a smaller pitch than the screw. A screw with a small pitch, with close threads, takes less force to drive than a screw with a greater pitch. However, with a small pitch, one turn of the screw only drives the screw a short distance into the wood. If the threads are farther apart, it takes more force to drive the screw, but the screw goes further into the wood with each turn. Again, we see the distance principle at work here. The mechanical advantage is paid for in distance.

Examine several items around you such as furniture, appliances, or anything with a handle. You will find wedges and screws used nearly everywhere. These simple machines make your life easier. ■

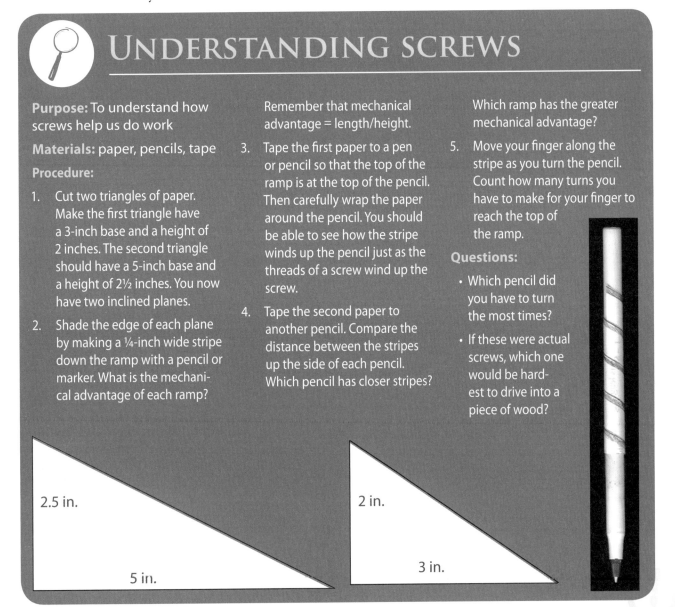

UNDERSTANDING SCREWS

Purpose: To understand how screws help us do work

Materials: paper, pencils, tape

Procedure:

1. Cut two triangles of paper. Make the first triangle have a 3-inch base and a height of 2 inches. The second triangle should have a 5-inch base and a height of 2½ inches. You now have two inclined planes.

2. Shade the edge of each plane by making a ¼-inch wide stripe down the ramp with a pencil or marker. What is the mechanical advantage of each ramp?

Remember that mechanical advantage = length/height.

3. Tape the first paper to a pen or pencil so that the top of the ramp is at the top of the pencil. Then carefully wrap the paper around the pencil. You should be able to see how the stripe winds up the pencil just as the threads of a screw wind up the screw.

4. Tape the second paper to another pencil. Compare the distance between the stripes up the side of each pencil. Which pencil has closer stripes?

Which ramp has the greater mechanical advantage?

5. Move your finger along the stripe as you turn the pencil. Count how many turns you have to make for your finger to reach the top of the ramp.

Questions:

- Which pencil did you have to turn the most times?

- If these were actual screws, which one would be hardest to drive into a piece of wood?

2.5 in.

5 in.

2 in.

3 in.

USING WEDGES

Purpose: To appreciate the usefulness of a wedge

Materials: pencil, cardboard

Procedure:

1. Using the flat eraser end of a sharpened pencil, try poking the pencil into a piece of cardboard. This will be very difficult. The pencil will probably flatten the cardboard, but will not puncture it.

2. Now turn the pencil around and try to poke the pencil into the cardboard with the pointed end. This is much easier because the point of the pencil is shaped like a wedge. This magnifies the effort at one point and allows the pencil to penetrate the cardboard.

3. With **adult supervision**, carefully observe several instruments with a wedge as their cutting edge. Do not touch the sharp edge, but look at how the blade slopes out away from the edge. This is the inclined plane that makes it easier to cut different materials.

WHAT DID WE LEARN?

- What is a wedge?
- How are wedges used in tools?
- What is a screw?
- How are screws used?
- What is the pitch of a screw?

TAKING IT FURTHER

- Which will be easier to drive into a piece of wood, a screw with 10 threads per inch or a screw with 15 threads per inch?
- Which of the above screws will go into the wood faster, assuming you have enough force to drive them both?
- Name at least two items with wedges that have not been mentioned in the lesson.

COMPARING SCREWS

Purpose: To compare different pitches of screws

Materials: two or more screws with different pitches, block of wood, screwdriver, tape measure, "Comparing Screws" worksheet

Procedure:

1. Examine each of the screws. How do the threads on the screws differ? Write your observations on the "Comparing Screws" worksheet.

2. Using a screwdriver, drive each screw into the wood a short distance. Which screw was easiest to drive? Which was most difficult?

3. Measure the height of each screw and write it on your worksheet.

4. Turn each screw ten turns of your wrist and measure the new height of each screw and write this down. The difference between the original height and the final height is the distance the screw went into the wood. Which screw went the furthest into the wood? Was this the screw that was easiest or hardest to drive?

5. Complete your worksheet.

Simple Machines

LEVERS

Seesaw

LESSON 12

How do levers help us do work?

Words to know:

lever

effort arm

fulcrum

resistance

effort

law of moments

How do people build skyscrapers or move tons of rock in a mine? Humans are not strong enough to move and do these things by themselves. Although God did not design our bodies with enough strength to move tons of rock, He did design our minds with enough imagination to design machines that can help us do things we could not do alone. You have already seen how inclined planes help people move objects, cut materials, and hold things together. A second simple machine that gives people mechanical advantage is the lever.

In simplest terms, a **lever** is a solid bar that rotates around a fixed point. You have probably played on a seesaw, which is a long piece of wood that rotates around a bar in the middle. This is a lever. A lever gives you mechanical advantage by allowing you to apply a force over a distance. This is the same distance principle that works with inclined planes.

To better understand how levers work, we need to define some terms and look at some examples. The solid bar of a lever is called the **effort arm**. The point around which the effort arm rotates is called the **fulcrum**. The weight that is being moved is called the **resistance** and the force that is being applied is called the **effort**.

An example will help you understand these terms. Think about the seesaw. The plank you sit on is the effort arm. The pole around which the plank rotates is the fulcrum. Your friend sitting on the opposite end is the resistance and your weight is the effort applied to move the resistance.

If the pole is in the exact middle of the plank and your friend sits on one end of the seesaw and you sit on the other end, the seesaw will balance if you both weigh the same amount. The resistance of your friend's weight and the

> **FUN FACT**
>
> Archimedes said, "Give me a long enough lever and a place to stand, and I can move the world." Because of the mass of the earth, this would require a very long lever indeed. Theoretically speaking, if you could make a lever long enough, you could lift any amount of weight. However, in practical terms, there is a limit to how long you can make a lever and still be able to use it.

effort of your weight are equal and are applied at equal distances from the fulcrum. Therefore the effort arm is balanced.

However, if your big brother sits on the other end instead of your friend and he weighs more than you do, you will go up in the air and he will sit on the ground. In order for you both to balance on the seesaw, your brother must move closer to the middle—closer to the fulcrum. Your effort must be applied at a farther distance from the fulcrum than the distance his weight is from the fulcrum.

In order to lift a heavy weight with a lever, the fulcrum should be placed near the weight and the effort should be applied at a greater distance. Less force is needed to lift the weight if the fulcrum is near the weight that is to be lifted, and the effort

EXPERIMENTING WITH LEVERS

Purpose: To understand how levers work

Materials: yardstick, block of wood, small box with heavy items

You can begin to appreciate levers by doing a few simple experiments. First, you need to make a lever. Use a stiff yardstick or meter stick as your effort arm. Use a small block of wood as your fulcrum. Fill a small box with sand, rocks, or other items to make it noticeably heavy to use as your resistance.

Activity 1: Procedure

1. Place the fulcrum in the center of the yardstick, at 18 inches (50 cm).

2. Place the box at one end of the yardstick.

3. Press down on the other end and lift the box.

4. Now, move the fulcrum so that it is 12 inches (30 cm) from the box and push down and lift the box. Was it easier or harder to lift the box?

5. Place the fulcrum 6 inches (15 cm) from the box and repeat. Was it easier or harder to lift the box this time?

6. Try placing the fulcrum 24 inches (70 cm) from the box. Push down and lift the box. Was it harder this time?

Activity 2: Procedure

1. Place the fulcrum 6 inches (15 cm) from the box and measure

the height of the end of the yardstick that you push on.

2. Push the yardstick all the way down and hold it there while you measure the height of the end of the yardstick with the box on it. Which moved farther, your hand or the box?

3. Repeat these measurements with the fulcrum at 12 inches, 18 inches, and 24 inches from the box. How does the distance your hand moved compare to the distance the box moved in each instance? Can you think of a reason why you might want to have the fulcrum at 24 inches from the box now?

Effort

Resistance

Effort arm

Fulcrum

is applied farther away. This is called the **law of moments**. If the effort is four times farther away from the fulcrum than the weight you want to lift, then you only have to apply one-fourth as much force to lift that weight. For example, if you want to lift a 200 pound rock, you could place a small rock one foot away from the large rock to use as a fulcrum. Then if you placed a sturdy pole over the small rock and under the big rock you now have a lever. If you pushed down four feet away from the small rock, you would only need to push down with 50 pounds of force instead of 200 pounds.

We have learned that mechanical advantage is paid for in distance. With respect to levers, this not only means that the effort must be applied at a greater distance from the fulcrum, but the real payment is the distance through which the effort is applied compared to the distance that the resistance moves. So if you are pushing down on one end of the lever and lifting a weight on the other end, the distance that you push down will be greater than the distance that the weight moves up. If the lever has a mechanical advantage of 4, then you must push down four times the distance that the weight will move up. You can push the lever down two meters and the weight will

A claw hammer provides leverage to pull a nail.

move up ½ meter. This is the payment for being able to push down with four times less effort.

Levers are used in many different ways. We will examine many different kinds of levers and ways that they are used in the next several lessons. ■

WHAT DID WE LEARN?

- What is a lever?

- How does a lever provide mechanical advantage?

- Define each of the following terms: effort arm, resistance, effort, fulcrum.

TAKING IT FURTHER

- How does the distance principle apply to levers?

- Give an example where you might want to apply a large force over a short distance in order to move an object over a large distance.

- When using a lever, do you do less work than if you lifted the object without the lever?

 LAW OF MOMENTS

The law of moments was first described mathematically by Archimedes. The law of moments states that $W_1 D_1 = W_2 D_2$ where W is the weight of the object and D is the distance from the fulcrum. This equation shows that the weight times the distance on one side must equal the weight

times the distance on the other side of the fulcrum. If you want to lift something that is twice as heavy with the same amount of force, you must move twice as far from the fulcrum.

We can calculate the mechanical advantage of the lever as $D_2 /$

D_1 where D_1 is the distance the resistance is from the fulcrum and D_2 is the distance the effort is from the fulcrum.

Using these two equations, complete the "Law of Moments" worksheet:

First-, Second-, & Third-Class Levers

What class are you in?

What different kinds of levers are there?

Words to know:

first-class lever

second-class lever

third-class lever

The levers we have studied so far have all been levers that have a weight or resistance at one end of the effort arm, the fulcrum somewhere in the middle, and the effort applied at the other end of the effort arm. This type of lever is called a **first-class lever**. First-class levers have been used to move heavy objects for thousands of years. In the previous lesson you saw the advantage of moving the fulcrum closer to the resistance.

Although first-class levers are the type you may be most familiar with, they are not the only kinds of levers. We classify other kinds of levers based on where the resistance is with respect to the fulcrum and the effort. A **second-class lever** has the fulcrum at one end, the resistance in the middle and the effort at the other end. The effort in this case would be applied as a lifting motion rather than as a pushing motion. The most familiar second-class lever is the wheelbarrow. The wheel is the fulcrum, the resistance sits in the middle of the wheelbarrow, and the effort is applied to the handles as the wheelbarrow is lifted up.

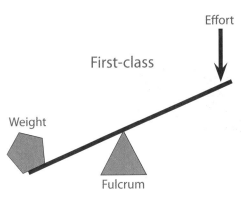

First-class

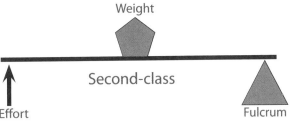

Second-class

CLASSIFYING LEVERS

Complete the "Lever Classification" worksheet.

Simple Machines

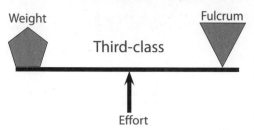

Weight

Fulcrum

Third-class

Effort

The third type of lever is the **third-class lever**. This lever has the fulcrum at one end, the effort applied in the middle and the resistance at the opposite end. A third-class lever that you use every day is your arm. Your elbow is the fulcrum of the lever. The muscle attached to the bone just below your elbow applies the force to move your lower arm and hand. And the weight of whatever is in your hand is the resistance that is being moved.

The advantage of the first- and second-class levers is fairly obvious. Less force is required to move the resistance even though the force must be applied over a greater distance. However, the advantage of the third-class lever may not be as obvious. A greater force is required to move the resistance than the weight of the resistance. However, the effort is applied over a shorter distance, allowing the resistance to be moved a longer distance in a shorter period of time. This is a great advantage when it comes to our bodies, giving us a greater field of motion.

Levers are used all around us, they just don't always look like you expect. Consider the wheelbarrow. Would you have thought of that as a lever? See if you can find other levers around your house. ■

The human arm is a third-class lever.

WHAT DID WE LEARN?

- Explain where the resistance, fulcrum, and effort are with respect to each other for each class of lever.

- Which class(es) of levers allow you to apply less effort to move an object?

- Which class(es) of levers allow you to move an object over a greater distance by applying more force?

TAKING IT FURTHER

- Which class(es) of levers will have a mechanical advantage less than 1? Which will be greater than 1?

- What kind of lever might you use if you want to prune a tree?

- What class of lever is a pencil?

- What advantage does a pencil give you?

Simple Machines

THIRD-CLASS LEVERS

To better understand levers and how they are used in various applications, complete the "Third-class Levers" worksheet.

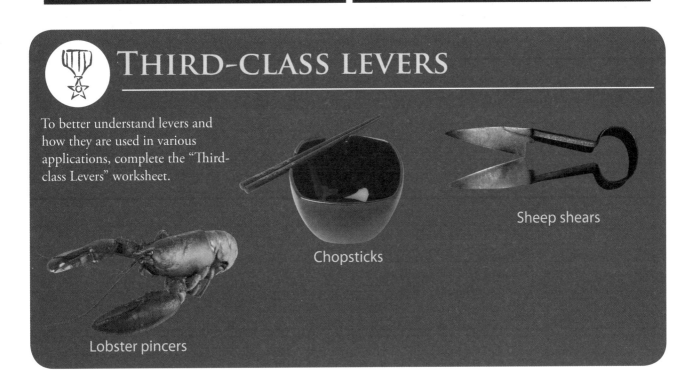

Sheep shears

Chopsticks

Lobster pincers

WHEELS & AXLES

Getting things moving

How do wheels and axles help us do work?

In the previous lesson we learned about three different classifications of levers. These various levers can make it easier to move something, but only over a limited distance. The blades of a pair of scissors can only move a few inches. A door can move a little further but is still limited. Even a catapult can only move the resistance a limited distance. However, levers have been modified into something that can be used to move objects an unlimited distance—the wheel and axle.

In a wheel and axle version of the lever, the center of the axle is the fulcrum. The effort arm and resistance arm rotate around the axle. This allows the resistance to be moved continuously. This modification of the lever is used to produce either mechanical advantage or distance advantage in a multitude of ways.

One common use of the wheel until recent history was the water wheel. The force of the water on the outside of a huge wheel was converted into a larger force to move various things such as a millstone to grind grain. Water wheels like the one pictured above were used in saw-mills, clothing mills, and many other capacities before electric motors became readily available.

A good example of how a wheel and axle combination increases your mechanical advantage is a fishing reel. The spool of fishing line is the resistance, especially when you have a fish on the end. The handle is the effort arm. Both of these rotate around the center of the axle. The handle is longer than the width of the spool, thus the effort is being applied farther from the

fulcrum. As you move the handle around, your hand will move a greater distance than the spool does. This gives you a mechanical advantage, thus allowing you to reel in a big fish with less effort. The longer the handle is compared to the width of the spool, the greater the mechanical advantage, but the more times you will have to turn the handle in order to reel in your catch.

A bicycle presents two different wheel-and-axle combinations. The first wheel is where the pedals are attached to the chain. The force from the pedals is transferred to the chain and a mechanical advantage is achieved. The force from the chain is applied to a second wheel—the rear wheel of the bicycle. This force is applied much closer to the axle than the force on the wheel. Thus, the advantage is not in less force but in a greater movement of the wheel. This allows your legs to move a relatively small distance while the wheel moves a greater distance.

Rear wheel gear

Pedal gear

Wheel and axle systems are extremely useful in many applications for increasing mechanical advantage or for increasing speed and distance traveled. However, wheels offer an additional advantage. Wheels are used on carts, automobiles, trailers, and many other forms of transportation because a wheel reduces the friction between the object being moved and the surface over which it is moving. Any particular point on the wheel is in contact with the surface of the road for only a short period of time, so resistance forces do not build up as much with a wheel as they do when two surfaces slide over each other. You can see that wheels are one of the most important inventions in history. ■

EXAMINING WHEELS

Carefully examine the various parts of a bicycle. Measure the distance from the pedal to the center of the axle about which is rotates. Next, measure the distance from the chain to the center of the axle. What is the mechanical advantage of the pedals to the chain?

Now examine the rear wheel of the bicycle. Measure the distance from the chain to the center of the rear axle. And measure the distance from the edge of the wheel to the center of the axle. What is the mechanical advantage at the rear wheel? This relationship is what allows the bike to move forward a large distance compared to the distance the pedals have moved.

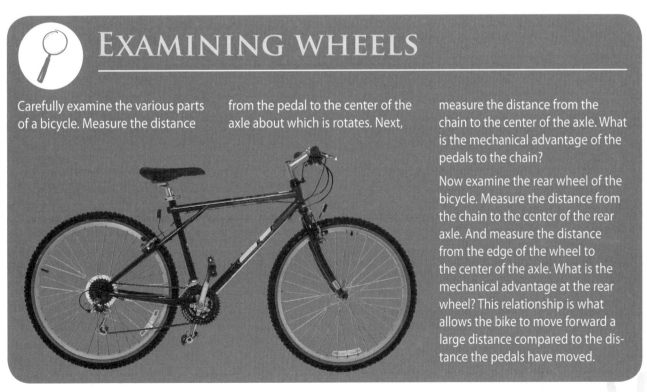

FUN FACT

A capstan is a rotating machine used to control or apply force to another element. Ships' capstans were traditionally manually operated, consisting of a shaped wooden drum (shown here) with handles inserted into the rim, at which men could push or pull. A capstan was used on ships to lift the anchor. A chain was wrapped around the axle and wound up, thus lifting up the heavy anchor. On land, a similar setup was sometimes used to haul heavy loads up a hill or out of a mine.

WHAT DID WE LEARN?

- A wheel and axle is a more complex version of which simple machine?
- What are the main reasons for using a wheel and axle instead of a regular lever?
- How does a wheel and axle increase mechanical advantage?

TAKING IT FURTHER

- How does a potter's wheel help the potter?

ROLLING FRICTION

Rolling friction is less than sliding friction because each point of the wheel touches the ground for only a short period of time then rises up, so there is very little friction. This is one reason why wheels make it easier to transport an object.

Purpose: To compare rolling and sliding friction

Materials: piece of wood, hook, rubber band, pencils

Procedure:

1. As you did in lesson 6, attach a rubber band to the hook in a piece of wood and drag it along the carpet. Observe how much the rubber band stretches.

2. Now, place several pencils close together on the floor.

3. Place the block of wood on top of the pencils and pull the wood across the pencils. Observe how much the rubber band stretches. It should be less than when the wood was on the carpet. Did the pencils roll? If not, add a weight to the top of the block and repeat the experiment.

Conclusion: You should notice a significant difference in the force required to move the block when it rolls on the pencils versus when it drags on the floor.

For an interesting research project, research the development of the spoked wheel.

Simple Machines

GEARS

Connecting wheels together

LESSON 15

How do gears help us do work?

Words to know:

gear

spur gear

bevel gear

rack and pinion

worm gear

When you examined a bicycle in the previous lesson, did you notice that the bike had more wheels involved than just the front and back tires? The pedals are attached to a wheel. That wheel is then attached to a special-looking wheel with teeth called a **gear**. The gear moves a chain. At the back of the bike, the chain moves a second gear that is in turn attached to the rear wheel. Are you starting to understand how a simple machine like the lever can be modified to make the various parts of a complex machine? A bicycle is an example of how a few simple gears and wheels can be connected to build a device to change a simple push of the foot into forward motion.

Gears are one of the most important types of levers for use in most machinery. Gears are wheels and axles with teeth along the outside edge. These teeth allow gears to move one another in a continuous way. The comparative size of the gears determines their function. Gears can be used to transfer mechanical advantage from one part of the machine to another. Smaller gears will rotate faster than larger gears, while larger gears exert a larger force than the smaller gears do. Thus, force and speed can be transferred in many different ways depending on the combination of gears used.

Let's look at a couple of examples. Consider if the gears shown here were connected together. If the force is applied to the larger gear, the smaller gear will rotate more quickly than the larger gear but will have less force. The mechanical advantage would be changed into speed. On the other hand, if the force is applied to the smaller gear, the larger gear will rotate more slowly but with a greater force. Speed would be changed into mechanical advantage.

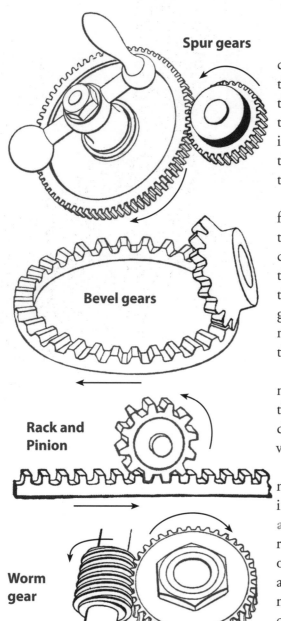

Spur gears

Bevel gears

Rack and Pinion

Worm gear

Larger and smaller gears working together can change the speed of the machine, either making something rotate more quickly or more slowly, by transferring the mechanical advantage of the wheels. This is the function of the transmission in a car. As the speed of the car increases, the transmission changes to a smaller gear so that the same force from the engine can make the wheels turn more quickly.

Gears can also be used to change the direction of a force. When two gears with parallel shafts are connected together they are called **spur gears**. If one gear rotates clockwise, the second gear rotates counter-clockwise, thus changing the direction of the rotation. If the rotation needs to be kept in the same direction as the original gear, but the speed needs to be changed, then a third gear needs to be added to the machine. This will cause the third gear to rotate in the same direction as the first gear.

Gears with non-parallel shafts can also be connected to each other. These are called **bevel gears**. If the gears are at right angles to each other this causes the direction of motion to be changed from horizontal to vertical or vise-versa.

Another use of gears in a machine is to change linear motion into rotational motion, or rotational motion into linear motion. This type of set up is called a **rack and pinion**. The pinion is a toothed wheel and the rack is a toothed bar that moves forward and backward or up and down with the rotation of the gear. A rack and pinion combination is used as the steering mechanism in many automobiles. A final type of gear set up is called a **worm gear**. A worm gear is a wheel that turns a threaded shaft.

Gears are used in nearly every machine. Because they are used in so many different ways, and often in rather complex ways, it is easy to forget that gears are really just modified levers. ■

FUN FACT

Early bicycles did not have gear and chain mechanisms like bicycles today. The early bikes had the pedals attached to the front wheel. Therefore, the front wheels of early bikes were very large compared to the back wheels to gain speed from the movement of the pedals.

PLAYING WITH GEARS

Purpose: To understand how gears work

Materials: cardboard, straight pins, "Gear Patterns" worksheet

Carefully trace each of the gear patterns from the worksheet onto a piece of thick cardboard and cut them out. Put a straight pin through the center of each gear to serve as an axle. You can stick the pins into a scrap piece of the cardboard to hold the gears in place.

Activity 1—Procedure:

1. Place gear A and gear B next to each other so they interlock.

2. Turn gear A and observe how gear B moves. Does A cause B to move faster or slower?

3. Now turn gear B and observe how gear A moves. Does B cause A to move faster or slower? If you wanted to move the wheels of your bike faster, would you use a larger gear to move a smaller gear or a smaller gear to move a larger gear?

Activity 2—Procedure:

1. Add gear C to gear B. Turn gear A. What direction do each of the gears move?

Activity 3—Procedure:

1. Place the rack next to gear A. Move gear A. How does the rack move?

2. Replace gear A with gear B. How does gear B move the rack differently than gear A did?

Activity 4—Procedure:

1. Experiment with different combinations of gears to see what different effects you can make. Scientists and engineers use great imagination in putting gears together to accomplish what they desire in a machine.

Simple Machines

WHAT DID WE LEARN?

- What is a gear?
- What are some functions that can be achieved with gear systems?
- In a gear system, in general, which will have the greater speed, the larger or smaller gear?
- Which will have the greater force, the larger or smaller gear?

TAKING IT FURTHER

- Why do most bicycles have more than one gear?
- How does putting a bicycle into a higher gear, one where the larger gear is driving the smaller gear, help a cyclist?
- How does putting a bicycle into a lower gear, one where the smaller gear is driving the larger gear, help a cyclist?

GEAR RESEARCH

There are four basic kinds of gear systems: rack and pinion, spur, bevel, and worm gears. Research a machine or your choice and find out what kinds of gear systems are used in it. Draw a diagram showing how the gears are used and describe their functions.

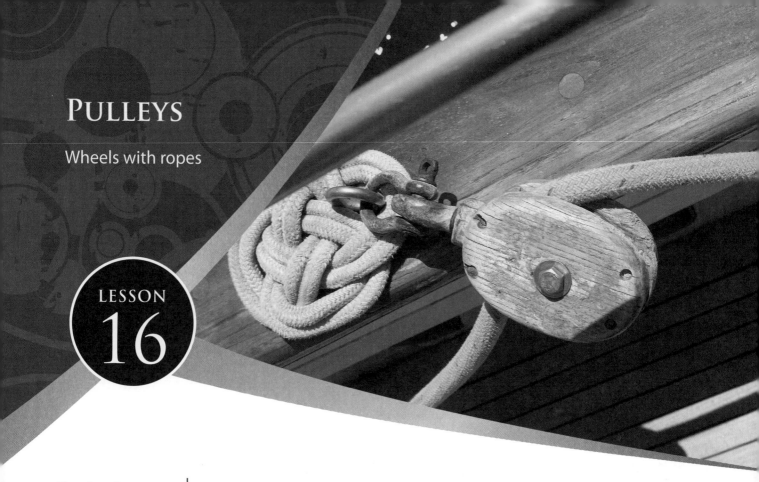

PULLEYS

Wheels with ropes

LESSON 16

How do pulleys help us do work?

Words to know:

block and tackle

Have you ever used a pulley? A pulley is another modification of the lever. A pulley is a grooved wheel that serves as the fulcrum of the lever. A rope is passed over the wheel. A resistance is attached to one end of the rope and an effort is applied to the other end of the rope. If the pulley is attached to the ceiling or some other immovable surface, the effort pulling down on the rope will move an equal weight in an upward direction. This may not seem like a useful machine because there is no mechanical advantage. However, because of the design of the human body, it is often easier to pull down than up, so even though the mechanical advantage of a single pulley is 1, it often seems easier to lift something with a pulley.

With a single fixed pulley, the distance that the effort moves the rope downward is equal to the distance that the resistance is moved upward. But more than one pulley can be used to improve the mechanical advantage. If a second pulley is added to the system, as shown here, the rope being pulled down moves twice as far as the weight moving upward. This gives the person pulling down on the rope a mechanical advantage of 2. A combination of fixed and moveable pulleys is called a **block and tackle**. The mechanical advantage of a block and tackle system is equal to the number of pulleys in the system. For example, if there are four pulleys in the system, the mechanical advantage is 4. Keep in mind that the person pulling the rope must pull it

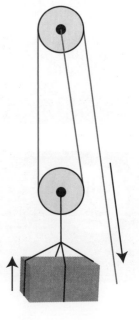

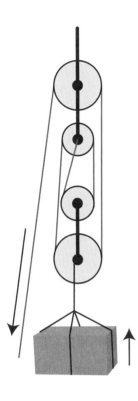

four times further than the height he wants to lift the weight.

Pulley systems are used in many machines today. A modern crane is an important use of a pulley system. Cranes allow us to lift very heavy objects, such as steel I-beams, into place on skyscrapers. Pulley systems also are used in elevators to lift the car up and down. And block and tackle systems have played a very important role on sailing ships for hundreds of years.

As you can see, the use of simple machines such as inclined planes, including screws and wedges, as well as levers in their many forms, including wheels, gears, and pulleys, make modern-day machines possible. Obviously, there are other technologies at work in many modern machines, including computer controls, but the mechanical movement of all complex machines is due to the use of these simple machines. ■

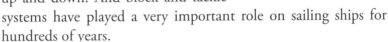

EXPERIMENTING WITH PULLEYS

Purpose: To experiment with pulleys

Materials: rope, 1-gallon jug, broom

Activity 1—1 fixed pulley

Procedure:

1. Attach one end of a rope to the handle of a 1-gallon jug of water.

2. Have someone hold a broom horizontally and loop the rope over the broom handle. Pull down on the rope to lift the jug. How much effort is required to lift the jug by pulling down on the rope compared to lifting it vertically without using the broom?

Activity 2—2 pulleys

Procedure:

1. Untie the rope from the handle of the jug and instead loop it through the handle and tie it to the broom.

2. Next, take the other end of the rope and loop it over the

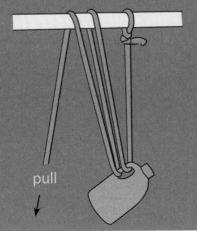

pull

broom handle. Pull down on the rope to lift the jug. How much effort is required to lift the jug compared to activity 1? How do you pay for this reduced effort?

Activity 3—4 pulleys

Procedure:

1. This time thread the rope through the handle of the jug, and over the broom handle a second time as shown in the picture here.

2. Again, pull on the rope to lift the jug. Does it feel easier than just lifting the jug alone? How far do you have to pull on the rope to lift the jug 1 foot off the ground? What is the mechanical advantage of this system?

WHAT DID WE LEARN?

- What is a pulley?
- What type of simple machine does a pulley represent?
- How does a pulley system provide a mechanical advantage?

TAKING IT FURTHER

- If someone wants to lift an object that is five times heavier than the person, what is the minimum number of pulleys needed in order for the person to be able to lift the object?
- How might a pulley system have been used in medieval warfare?
- In lesson 9 you were asked to identify simple machines around you. Now that you have learned more about simple machines, go back and look at the same objects and see if you can identify more simple machines.

MECHANICAL ADVANTAGE

The mechanical advantage of a pulley system can be determined by the number of ropes that are supporting the weight of the object being lifted. A single fixed pulley has a mechanical advantage of 1. Examine the pictures below. For each pulley system, determine the mechanical advantage.

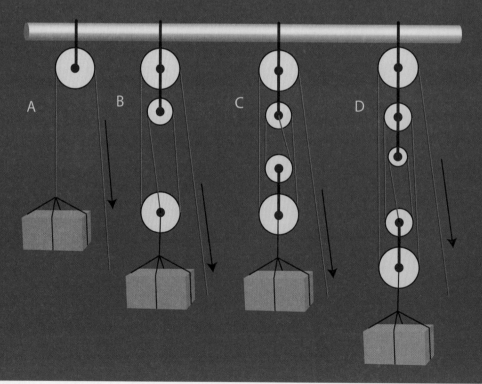

UNIT 3

KINEMATICS

◊ **Describe** how reference points change observations of motion.

◊ **Distinguish** between speed, velocity, and acceleration.

◊ **Relate** basic concepts of special relativity.

17 Kinematics • 58

18 Speed & Velocity • 60

19 Acceleration • 63

20 Theory of Relativity • 66

KEY CONCEPTS | UNIT LESSONS

KINEMATICS

How do things move?

LESSON
17

What affects how things move?

Words to know:

kinematics

frame of reference

relative motion

How would you describe the movement of a car? Is it moving fast or slow? Is it traveling north? Maybe it is slowing down. All of these words describe movement and are used in kinematics. **Kinematics** is the study of how things move. It is the study of speed, velocity, and acceleration.

At the beginning of the book you were asked to sit very still and not move. When you are sitting like this, how fast are you moving? You probably think you are not moving at all. And from one point of view you are correct. But if someone (like an astronaut) could observe you from a point in space above the earth, he would say that you are moving very quickly. This is because the earth is rotating on its axis, and you are moving with the earth. Also, the earth is revolving around the sun and again you are moving through space with the earth. So, you see you are not really sitting still. Movement is relative—it depends on your perspective. This perspective is called **frame of reference**.

In the past, many people believed that the sun, moon, and stars moved around the earth, but that the earth was stationary. They believed this because this is what they could observe. It is what they seemed to see. From the frame of reference of the earth, the sun, moon, and stars were moving with respect to the earth. Careful observation of other planets and stars helped scientists determine that all of the heavenly bodies are moving with respect to each other, including the earth. All of these observations show us that movement is relative. It depends on your frame of reference.

Another example may better help you understand frame of reference. If you are standing on a sidewalk and a car goes by, you will observe that the passenger is moving quickly past you. However, if you were a passenger in the car, the other passenger would not be moving at all with respect to you. In our study of motion, it is very

FRAME OF REFERENCE

Purpose: To understand frame of reference

Materials: stuffed animal, wagon

Procedure:

1. Place a stuffed animal in a wagon.

2. Stand in one place and have someone pull the wagon in a line in front of you so the wagon moves from your left to your right. How did the wagon appear to move? How did the stuffed animal appear to move?

3. Next, place the stuffed animal on the ground where you were standing. You sit in the wagon and have someone pull you over the same path. How does the wagon appear to move now? (Be sure to look only at the wagon.) How does the stuffed animal appear to move?

important to define our frame of reference. We must define motion of one object as being with respect to another object. This is called relative motion. There is no fixed frame of reference so there is no absolute or correct description of motion. In general, if a frame of reference is not specified, it is assumed that the movement is being described with respect to the person making the observations and that the person is somewhere on the earth.

Frame of reference is the first thing we must understand when studying kinematics. If we do not understand our frame of reference, we cannot adequately define how the object is moving. Once we define the frame of reference, we can examine the object's speed, velocity, acceleration, and other aspects of how it moves. ■

WHAT DID WE LEARN?

- What is kinematics?
- What is frame of reference?
- What is relative motion?

TAKING IT FURTHER

- Why is it important to define your frame of reference when discussing motion?

- If an observer were outside the Milky Way galaxy and could observe the earth, what types of motion would the earth appear to be making?

- If a child on a moving train is tossing a ball and catching it, how does the ball appear to move from the child's point of view? How does it appear to move to an observer standing on the ground outside the train?

FRAME OF REFERENCE

Thinking about frame of reference may seem pretty easy when we look at the things that are moving around us. However, it becomes more complicated when we consider frames of reference outside the surface of the earth. Think about how things would appear to move as you complete the "Frame of Reference" worksheet.

Kinematics

SPEED & VELOCITY

How fast are you going?

LESSON

18

What is the difference between speed and velocity?

Words to know:

speed

velocity

Challenge words:

vector

magnitude

One of the first things scientists look at when trying to describe movement is the speed at which something is moving. **Speed** is the rate at which something changes position with respect to something else. Speed is sometimes called rate.

The length that something moves is called the distance. The faster something is moving the less time it will take to cover a certain distance. Thus, speed is the distance covered divided by the time it takes to go that distance. For example, if your car is moving at 30 miles per hour, in one hour the car will have covered a distance of 30 miles. But if the car is moving at 60 mph, it will cover twice the distance in the same amount of time. Although Americans are used to cars moving in units called miles per hour, the standard scientific unit for speed is meters per second (m/s), so scientific measurements measure speed using these units.

If you know the speed of an object and the length of time it has been moving, you can calculate the distance it has traveled. Likewise, if you know the distance and the speed, you can determine how long it would take. For example, if you are riding

MEASURING SPEED & VELOCITY

Purpose: To measure speed and velocity with a few simple instruments

Materials: sidewalk chalk, meter stick, stopwatch, compass

Procedure:

1. Using sidewalk chalk or tape, mark a starting line.

2. Use a meter stick or tape measure to measure out 10 meters, 25 meters, and 50 meters from the starting point, and mark each of these distances with tape or chalk.

3. Have one person use a stopwatch to time how long it takes for you to run to each mark.

4. Write down each time and calculate your speed. Remember that speed is distance divided by time.

5. Now determine your velocity by using a compass to determine the direction in which you were running.

your bike at 10 m/s and you ride for 300 seconds, you will travel a distance of 3,000 meters. Similarly, it will take you 100 seconds to go 1,000 meters if you ride your bike at a speed of 10 m/s.

Quite often, objects will not move at a consistent speed over a long period of time. If you are riding your bike, you may slow down going up a hill and go faster down a hill than you do on a flat surface. Similarly, a car cannot maintain a consistent speed because of stop lights and changes in traffic. So, quite often a speed calculation will determine the average speed of an object instead of the actual speed. If you ride your bike 4.5 km (4,500 m) to your friend's house in 15 minutes (900 seconds) your average speed will be 4,500 m/900 sec = 5 m/s. But you probably went faster and slower than 5 m/s during different parts of your ride.

Another important measurement used to describe an object's movement is velocity. Many people think that speed and velocity are the same thing. But from a scientific point of view there is an important difference. Speed describes how much distance is covered in a particular time period. But **velocity** describes the direction as well as the speed of an object. When describing the velocity of an airplane, the velocity would be given as traveling westward at 200 m/s, for example, but its speed would just be 200 m/s without a direction attached. Velocity gives us more information about how an object is moving than just the speed alone. Velocity is an important measurement in determining where an object goes as it moves. ■

WHAT DID WE LEARN?

- What is the definition of speed?
- What are the standard units for speed?
- How is velocity different from speed?

TAKING IT FURTHER

- Why is it important to know an object's velocity instead of just its speed?
- What kind of instruments might be needed to measure speed and velocity?

VECTORS

Velocity is a **vector** quantity. This means that it can be represented by an arrow. The length of the arrow is called the **magnitude** and it represents the speed of the object. The faster the object is going, the longer the arrow will be. And since velocity must include direction information, the direction the arrow is pointing represents the direction the object is moving.

An example will help you understand what we are talking about. Consider an airplane flying north at 200 mph. We could draw the airplane's velocity by a line that is 2 inches long pointing straight up. Now let's say that the wind is blowing from the east at 20 mph causing the airplane to move toward the west at 20 mph. We can use an arrow to represent the movement of the plane due to the wind. This arrow would be ¹⁄₁₀ as long as the other arrow, or 0.2 inches long, and would point to the left.

The advantage of using arrows, or vectors, to represent velocity is that the vectors can be added together to determine the actual speed and direction of the plane. When the vector representing the velocity of the plane is combined with the vector showing the velocity due to the wind, an arrow is drawn, as you see here, showing the actual speed and direction of the plane. The plane is actually moving slightly to the northwest.

Vectors are very useful for describing and calculating the final movement of objects that are affected by more than one force. Computers on airplanes, boats, and other vehicles use these vector quantities to help them keep track of the actual location of the vehicle so the pilot can compensate for the wind or current and end up at the correct destination. In this instance, if the plane needed to fly to a destination that was due north, the pilot needs to fly north and slightly east to compensate for the wind. Computer programs are designed to take these factors into consideration and plot an appropriate course.

To get practice understanding vectors, complete the "Vectors" worksheet.

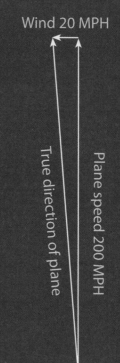

Wind 20 MPH

True direction of plane

Plane speed 200 MPH

Kinematics

ACCELERATION

Speeding up

LESSON 19

How do we measure acceleration?

Words to know:

acceleration

deceleration

How fast are you moving when you first start riding your bicycle? Are you moving faster after you have been pedaling for a few seconds? As we mentioned before, you do not move at a constant rate when you ride your bicycle. Sometimes you go faster and other times you go slower, so your speed is changing.

The rate at which an object's speed is changing is called acceleration if the object's speed is becoming greater, and deceleration if the object's speed is slowing down. Because acceleration is a rate, it is measured as a change over time. So acceleration is defined as the change in speed or velocity over time.

If you are riding your bike at three meters per second and you come to the top of a hill, you will speed up as you go down the hill if you do not apply your brakes. Let's say that it takes you four seconds to reach the bottom of the hill, and at the bottom of the hill you are going 5 m/s. Your speed has changed from 3 m/s to 5 m/s. This is a change of 2 m/s. The time it took to make this change was four seconds. So your acceleration was 2 m/s divided by four seconds, which is 0.5 m/s^2.

If you had been riding up the hill instead of down the hill and your speed decreased from 3 m/s to 1 m/s in a four second time period, then your deceleration would be −0.5 m/s^2. We use the negative sign to show that the speed became less and you experienced deceleration.

MEASURING ACCELERATION

Purpose: To observe the acceleration caused by gravity

Materials: toy car, long piece of wood, cardboard, stopwatch, marker, tape

Procedure:

1. Construct a ramp by using a long piece of wood. An 8 foot long piece of a 2x4 works well. Add side rails by taping cardboard to each side of the wood. Prop up one end of the wood to form the ramp.

2. Place a toy car at the top of the ramp and release it.

3. Have one person watch a stopwatch and call out each second that the car is traveling. Have a second person make a mark on the cardboard showing where the car was at each second.

4. Measure the distance that the car rolled each second.

Conclusion: You should see that the distance the car traveled in the first second is less than the distance that the car traveled in the next second and so on. This shows that the car was traveling faster after two seconds than it was after one second. This is because the force of gravity is causing it to accelerate.

Objects can accelerate and decelerate for many reasons. A force exerted on an object in the same direction in which it is traveling will increase its velocity. When you are riding your bike, you are adding force by pedaling. The harder you pedal, the faster you will accelerate. An automobile will increase its speed when the driver adds more force by pressing down the accelerator, which increases the amount of fuel being used and increases the force on the wheels. Gravity is a force that is constantly pulling down on objects. It causes falling objects to increase in velocity. We will study this increase in velocity when we take a closer look at the effects of gravity in lesson 24.

Objects will decelerate when a force is applied that opposes the movement of the object. When you apply your brakes to your bike, the friction opposes the forward motion of the wheels and causes you to slow down. When you drive a car up a hill, gravity is opposing your upward motion. Your speed will decrease if you do not press harder on the accelerator. The car will experience deceleration.

Let's review the terms that help us describe an object's movement. Speed is the distance covered in a given period of time. Velocity is the speed of the object and the direction in which it is moving. And acceleration is the change in velocity over a given period of time, or the rate at which the speed/velocity is changing. And don't forget that all of this motion is relative to your frame of reference! ∎

WHAT DID WE LEARN?

- What is acceleration?
- What is the difference between acceleration and deceleration?
- What causes an object to accelerate?
- What causes an object to decelerate?

TAKING IT FURTHER

- When a runner is in a sprint race, is there a time when the runner is neither accelerating nor decelerating?
- What happens to the speed of an object that is accelerating?

Kinematics

ACCELERATION GRAPH

Purpose: To visualize acceleration by making a graph

Materials: "Acceleration" worksheet

Procedure:

1. Using the "Acceleration" worksheet, calculate the actual velocity of the car during each second it traveled down the ramp. Remember that velocity is distance over time in a given direction.

2. On your worksheet, make a graph of acceleration. Label the x-axis "Time" in seconds, and the y-axis "Velocity" in meters per second.

3. Place a point on the graph showing the velocity of the car at 1 second, 2 seconds, etc. Then connect the dots.

Conclusion: Depending on the length of your ramp and the speed of the car, you may have only 2 or 3 points on your graph. The line should go up and to the right. This line represents the acceleration of the car.

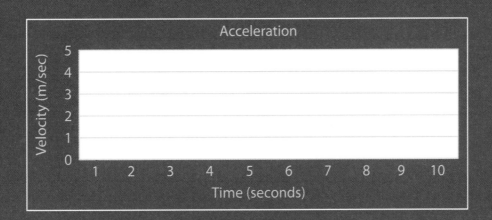

Assuming that the ramp was long enough, use your graph to predict the speed of the car after 4 seconds, 5 seconds, and 6 seconds.

Would you expect the graph to be a straight line? Why or why not?

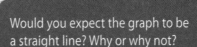

Acceleration graph — y-axis: Velocity (m/sec) with values 0, 1, 2, 3, 4, 5; x-axis: Time (seconds) with values 1 through 10.

THEORY OF RELATIVITY

Is everything relative?

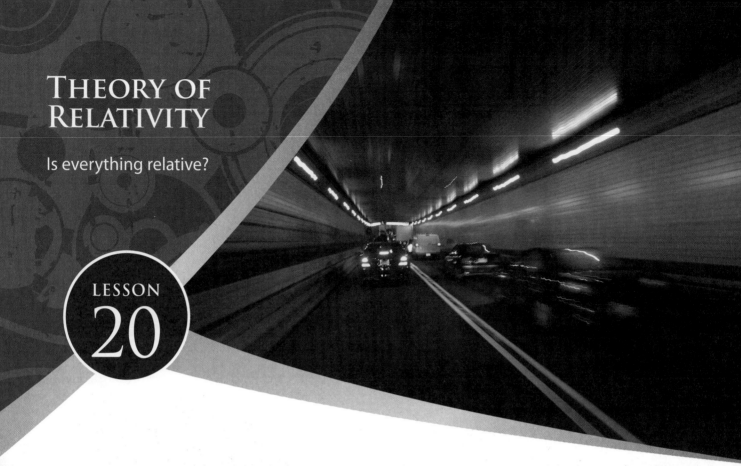

What is the Special Theory of Relativity?

When we think of moving objects, we consider their relative velocities and their acceleration. By observing the way everyday objects move it is pretty easy to understand relative velocity. For example, if a person is in a car moving north at 50 mph and a car is traveling south toward that person at 50 mph, the car going south is approaching the person at a relative velocity of 100 mph. From the person's frame of reference inside the northbound car, the southbound car appears to be traveling twice as fast as it would appear to someone outside both vehicles.

This relative velocity seems to be true for all objects that we observe around us. However, Albert Einstein observed that this is not true for light. In 1905, Einstein published his Special Theory of Relativity. Among other observations, Einstein showed that as objects approach the speed of light they behave differently than expected. Take our car example. If light is approaching the northbound car at 186,000 miles per second (300,000 km/s), which is the speed of light in a vacuum, to the observer it should appear to approach at that speed plus 50 miles per hour. However, the light still only appears to approach at the regular speed of light. In essence, the speed of light is a true speed limit. Nothing seems to be able to go faster than the speed of light.

FUN FACT

In 1971 an experiment was conducted which tried to prove Einstein's theory. Extremely sensitive atomic clocks were placed on a very high-speed aircraft and flown around the earth. The time on the clocks was then compared with the time on the clocks that remained on the earth. The flown clocks were slower by 0.0000001 seconds. This may seem like a minimal amount, but it was enough for scientists to claim that Einstein was right.

RELATIVITY POSTER

Make a poster advertising the "Special Theory of Relativity." Try to include as many of the following ideas as possible.

- $E = mc^2$

- The speed of light is 186,000 miles per second (300,000 km/s)
- Time slows down as you approach the speed of light

- Mass increases as you approach the speed of light
- Nothing can go faster than the speed of light

Have fun and use your imagination!

Thus, the velocity of light is not relative to the frame of reference.

In order for this to be true, Einstein showed that time is relative as objects approach the speed of light. If someone were able to travel on a rocket at a speed near the speed of light, time would pass more slowly for that person than for the person on earth. The person on earth would age more quickly than the person on the rocket. This idea has been fuel for many science fiction stories, although it is not possible for a person to travel at anything close to the speed of light.

Einstein's theory also included the idea that matter can be transformed into energy. This has been shown to be true with the development of nuclear energy. A small amount of uranium is transformed, releasing huge amounts of energy in a nuclear reactor. Einstein described this relationship in his famous equation $E = mc^2$. The energy released is equal to the mass times the speed of light squared. The speed of light is very fast so the amount of energy contained in a small amount of mass is very large.

Finally, Einstein's Special Theory of Relativity shows that the mass of an object increases as it approaches the speed of light. This is hard to visualize because mass seems to be independent of speed. However, according to the theory, at speeds approaching the speed of light, an object's mass increases. This makes it very difficult to accelerate objects to very high speeds. The only things known to be able to travel at the speed of light are electromagnetic waves, which include light, X-rays, and gamma rays. ■

WHAT DID WE LEARN?

- Who developed the Special Theory of Relativity?
- What are some main ideas of the Special Theory of Relativity?

TAKING IT FURTHER

- Why is it difficult and likely impossible for an object to travel at the speed of light?
- If it were possible to travel at or near the speed of light, who would age faster, a person on earth or a person traveling in a rocket near the speed of light?

RELATIVE MOTION OF LIGHT

In 1887 Albert Michelson and Edward Morley performed an experiment in which a beam of light was split so that one part traveled at a 90-degree angle to the other part of the beam. These two beams were then brought together again. Would you expect the two beams to line up with each other? Consider the frame of reference for the traveling beams of light. One of the beams was traveling in the same direction as the motion of the earth and the other beam was traveling at a 90-degree angle to that motion. Recall the example of throwing a ball on the train. From the frame of reference of the train, the ball moves up and down, but from the frame of reference outside the train the ball moves in an arc. Therefore, you would expect that the beams would not line up. However, the beams lined up nearly perfectly, showing that the speed of light was not dependent on the motion of the earth. Is your motion dependent on the motion of the earth? Yes, you are moving at the same speed as the earth. Albert Einstein's Special Theory of Relativity helped to explain the results of this experiment.

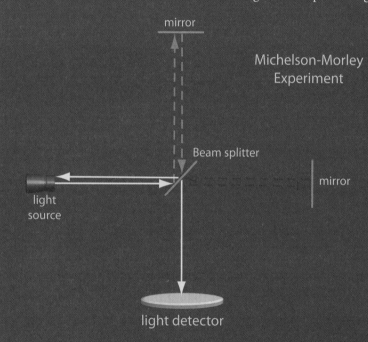

Michelson-Morley Experiment

mirror

Beam splitter

mirror

light source

light detector

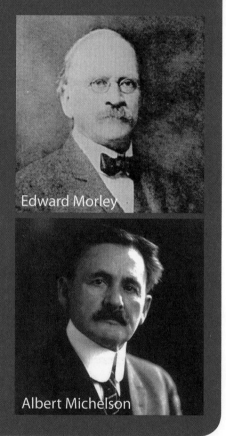

Edward Morley

Albert Michelson

FUN FACT

Einstein's General Theory of Relativity predicts that space and time are distorted by the presence of massive objects. From 2004 to 2005 NASA conducted an experiment called Gravity Probe B (GP-B), which used very sensitive gyroscopes to accurately measure two effects: 1) the geodetic effect—the amount by which the earth warps the local space-time in which it resides; and 2) the frame-dragging effect—the amount by which the rotating earth drags its local space-time around with it. The results of the experiment confirmed Einstein's predictions to within 1%.

ALBERT EINSTEIN

1879–1955

"Try not to become a man of success but rather to become a man of value."

When you hear the name Albert Einstein do you picture a wild-haired man? Do you think of the Theory of Relativity? This is what most people think of, but there is much more to Albert Einstein.

Albert Einstein was born on March 14, 1879, in Ulm, Germany. His interest in science may have started when he was about four or five years old when he saw his first "wonder" of science—a compass. He was very impressed by the invisible force that made the needle always point back to north. According to members of his family, Albert was a slow talker at first, always considering what he would say. When he was still very young, he started his education. He learned the violin and he also had religious studies in Judaism until he was thirteen. Two people who helped stimulate his mind were his uncle, who was an engineer, and a medical student who ate dinner with the family once a week.

At the age of thirteen, Albert started attending the Luitpold Gymnasium in Munich where he continued his religious studies and later went on to study mathematics, in particular calculus. Much of his real learning took place at home where he studied physics, math, and philosophy. In 1895 Einstein failed an examination that would have allowed him to study in Zurich for an electrical engineering degree. But he later was admitted to the University of Zurich where he studied mathematics and physics.

In 1896 Einstein renounced his German citizenship and moved to Switzerland. However, he did not apply for Swiss citizenship until 1899, and citizenship was not granted until 1901. So he was stateless for about five years.

It was during his time in Zurich that Albert met Mileva Maric, who would later become his wife and helper. Mileva was quite the prodigy. At age fifteen she got special permission to take classes at an all-male prep school. She kept to herself and earned the highest grades in both math and physics. In 1896 she changed her university path from medicine to the university's Technical Institute. She was only the fifth woman to be admitted to the school. Here she met Albert. She was 21 and Albert was only 17. Her first year she did very well at school. Then, she spent the first semester of her second year in Heidelberg and exchanged letters with Albert.

Mileva returned to Zurich in the spring of 1899 and the romance continued. The time spent together had an impact on both of them, as both failed their final exams. Einstein was still able to get his diploma but had no job. Mileva was from a well-off family and she supported him while he looked for a job.

Einstein was unable to get permanent work at the university and ended up working at the Swiss patent office. Albert and Mileva were married on January 6, 1903, but spent much of their time apart. During their times apart they kept in touch by mail. Many of these letters talked about physics, in particular the work for which Einstein received the Nobel Prize. It would appear that Albert's wife was involved in this work. In fact, in 1905, after they were married and had two children, she wrote to one of her friends, "We finished some important work that will make my husband world famous." That year Einstein published four papers, and he received his doctorate from the University of Zurich for one of those papers.

The hard work he and his wife did together paid off. In 1908 Einstein became a lecturer at the University of Bern and the next year he became the professor of physics at the University of Zurich. This allowed him to resign his lectureship and his job at the patent office. He became a German citizen again in 1914, and he was appointed director of the Kaiser Wilhelm Physical Institute and professor at the University of Berlin. Then in 1921, Einstein received the Nobel Prize for Physics. Most people assume that this was awarded for his Theory of Relativity. However, he actually received the prize for the work he had done in 1905 on the photoelectric effect.

In the 1920s Einstein began working for the Zionist cause, which was pushing for a homeland for the Jews in Palestine. He traveled around the world to raise money for Zionism and for Hebrew University in Jerusalem, where he served as governor of the university from 1925–1928.

During one trip to the United States, he was offered a professorship at Princeton, which he accepted. While working at Princeton in 1933, the Nazis took over Germany and Einstein again renounced his German citizenship. In 1940 he became a U.S. citizen but also retained his Swiss citizenship. In 1944 he helped the war effort by allowing a hand-written copy of his 1905 paper on special relativity to be auctioned off. The paper raised 6 million dollars and is now in the Library of Congress. He retired his post at Princeton in 1945.

By this time Einstein was looked upon as one of the leading world political figures. In 1952, after the death of Israel's first president, Einstein was offered the position as the second president of Israel. He turned down this offer, however. Einstein died on April 18, 1955, and his body was cremated with the ashes scattered at an undisclosed place. He left his papers to Hebrew University.

UNIT 4

DYNAMICS

◊ **Define**, with examples, the three laws of motion.

◊ **Describe** how gravity affects the motion of objects.

◊ **Explain** the behavior of falling bodies.

◊ **Describe** how to find an object's center of mass.

KEY CONCEPTS

21 First Law of Motion • 72

22 Second Law of Motion • 75

23 Third Law of Motion • 78

24 Gravity • 80

25 Falling Bodies • 84

26 Center of Mass • 87

UNIT LESSONS

FIRST LAW OF MOTION

Inertia

What is inertia and how does it affect motion?

Words to know:

dynamics

inertia

law of inertia

first law of motion

Dynamics

We have been studying how things move. We have learned that moving objects have a velocity. They move at a particular speed in a particular direction. We have also learned that objects can accelerate. If they are accelerating, they are moving faster over time. If they are decelerating, they are moving more slowly over time. We have also learned that an object's motion is relative depending on your frame of reference. Now that we understand how objects move, let's take a look at why objects move the way they do. The study of why objects move is called **dynamics**.

When you studied about acceleration, you saw that a toy car accelerates down a ramp then slows down and stops. People have always observed that objects around them slow down and stop if no force is applied to keep them going. Because of this, many people believed that an object needs to have a constant force applied to it in order for it to keep moving. This seems like a logical conclusion. However, this is not the case.

Two important scientists studied how and why objects move and discovered that an object needs a force to get it moving, but once it is moving it will not stop unless a force is applied in the opposite direction to make it stop. Galileo was one of the first scientists to propose this idea. His studies convinced him that forces were not needed to keep an object in motion. Sir Isaac Newton expanded on these studies and established what are called Newton's laws of motion. There are three laws of motion and they explain why objects move the way they do.

Newton discovered that all objects have inertia.

Sir Isaac Newton

OBSERVING INERTIA

Purpose: To observe Newton's first law of motion

Materials: ball, wagon, cup, table, playing card, coin

Activity 1—Procedure :

1. Place a ball in the center of a wagon and begin pulling the wagon. What happens to the ball? At first it will appear to roll to the back of the wagon. This is because the ball wants to stay at rest even after the wagon begins to move. Eventually, the friction with the wagon and contact with the back of the wagon will force the ball to begin moving with the wagon.

2. Once the ball is moving with the wagon, quickly stop the wagon. What happens to the ball? Why did the ball roll to the front of the wagon? The ball had inertia that keeps it moving forward even after the wagon stops moving.

Conclusion: Have you ever ridden in a bumper car at an amusement park? Your body experiences motion similar to the ball in the wagon. You are moving forward with the car when suddenly some- one hits the side of your car with his and changes the direction of your car. Your body slides to one side with respect to the car because your inertia is carrying you in the same direction you were moving before the collision.

Activity 2—Procedure :

1. Place a cup of water on a table and set a playing card on top of the cup.

2. Place a coin on top of the card.

3. Flick the edge of the card with your finger hard enough to make it move off of the cup. What happened to the coin? Why did the coin fall into the cup?

Conclusion: The coin's inertia made it want to stay still even when the card started to move. The card was slippery enough that there was not much friction between the card and the coin. Then the coin fell because gravity pulled it down. If you pay attention, you will see iner- tia at work all around you.

Inertia is an object's tendency to stay in the condition it is in. This means that an object that is not moving does not start moving without an outside force being applied, and an object that is moving does not stop moving without an outside force being applied. This is often called the **law of inertia** or Newton's **first law of motion**. The first law of motion is often stated as, "an object at rest will remain at rest and an object in motion will remain in motion unless acted upon by an outside force."

It is pretty easy to recognize that an object at rest stays at rest. We do not see books just suddenly moving across the table or chairs moving themselves across the

FUN FACT

In outer space there is no air resistance or friction so objects that are put in motion stay in motion. For example, NASA sent the Voyager space probes into space in the 1970s. There has been no additional force added to the probes in many years, yet they are still traveling through space and will continue to do so until something gets in the way to stop them.

floor. However, the other half of the law is less obvious. It seems that moving objects do stop by themselves. When you rolled a toy car down a ramp, the car stopped without your help. This is because there are unseen forces acting on the car. The air molecules are pushing against the car causing it to slow down. Also, friction between the car's wheels and the floor is another force acting to slow the car down. Galileo and Newton understood that in an ideal environment, one with no friction or air resistance, the toy car would continue moving in a straight line forever if there was nothing in its way to stop it. ■

WHAT DID WE LEARN?

- What is inertia?
- What is Newton's first law of motion?

TAKING IT FURTHER

- How will an object move if the forces acting on it are balanced—they are equal but in opposite directions?

- When you jump you come down in about the same place on the floor. Since the earth is rotating on its axis, why don't you land in a different place as the earth moves under you?

- Since a stopped car wants to stay at rest, what force makes a car move?

- Is more gasoline needed to get a car moving to begin with, or to keep the car moving at a constant speed?

BALANCED FORCES

According to Newton's first law of motion, an object at rest tends to stay at rest and an object in motion tends to stay in motion unless acted upon by an outside force. In order to overcome an object's inertia, there must be an unbalanced force.

Think back to when we talked about a suspension bridge. There are forces acting on the bridge, yet it does not move. Gravity is pulling down on the bridge and

the tension in the cable is pulling up on the bridge. These forces are equal so the bridge does not move. However, if something happened to increase or decrease one of the forces, the bridge would move. For example, if the cable were cut there would no longer be an upward force, but only a downward force; the forces would be unbalanced so the bridge would fall. Can you think of other objects that are not moving because the forces acting on them are balanced?

Newton's first law of motion can be fun. You can use it to determine whether an egg is raw or hardboiled without opening the egg. Design a test that uses inertia to help you figure out which egg is cooked. Use your test to see if it works.

Dynamics

SECOND LAW OF MOTION

It's all about force

How are force and mass related to acceleration?

Words to know:

second law of motion

law of acceleration

Dynamics

Have you ever tried to push a big rock or pick up a heavy box? Was it hard to do? Moving a heavy object is harder than moving a light object. This is the idea behind Newton's **second law of motion**. The second law states that the net force required to move an object is equal to the object's mass multiplied by its acceleration:

$$F = ma$$

This may sound difficult, but let's look at what this really means. First, inertia is directly related to the mass of the object. Mass is how much substance the object has. The more massive something is, the more it resists change. A large boulder has more mass than a small pebble so it has more inertia. Therefore, more force is required to move a boulder than to move a pebble if we want them both to have the same acceleration.

If we look at this relationship from the acceleration point of view instead of from the force point of view, we see that if an equal force is applied to two objects, the object with the least mass will experience the greater acceleration. For example, if you throw a baseball and a bowling ball with the same force, the baseball will fly much faster than the bowling ball. Its smaller mass results in greater acceleration.

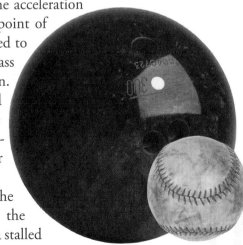

Newton's second law also tells us the more force that is applied to an object, the faster it will accelerate. Consider pushing a stalled

TESTING NEWTON'S SECOND LAW

Purpose: To observe Newton's second law of motion

Materials: masking tape, two roller skates, hammer, can of food

Activity 1—Procedure:

1. Place a piece of masking tape on the floor to mark the starting line.

2. Place a roller skate at the starting line.

3. Using a hammer, give the skate a small tap on the back. Observe how fast it moves.

4. Replace the skate at the starting line and this time tap it harder. How did the skate move the second time compared to the first time?

Conclusion: The skate should move much faster the second time because you applied a greater force, so the skate accelerated more quickly. The mass was the same each time, so the increased force is what caused the increased acceleration.

Activity 2—Procedure:

1. Place two skates at the starting line and add a can of food or other heavy object to one skate. The skate with the can now has more mass than the skate without the can.

2. Tap the lighter skate with a hammer and observe its motion.

3. Tap the heavier skate with a hammer. Try to use the same amount of force. What difference did you observe in the heavier skate's motion?

Conclusion: The heavier skate should move more slowly because of its additional mass. With equal force, the object with the greater mass experiences less acceleration.

car off of the road. If one person pushes the car by himself, the car will move very slowly. But if three or four people work together, they can apply a greater force and the car will accelerate much more quickly. Because Newton's second law describes the acceleration of an object with respect to its mass and the force applied to it, this law is sometimes called the **law of acceleration**. ■

WHAT DID WE LEARN?

- What is the equation that expresses Newton's second law of motion?

- What is another name for the second law of motion?

- If the same force is applied to two objects with different masses, what will be the effect on their accelerations?

- If you wish to increase the acceleration of an object, how must the force change?

TAKING IT FURTHER

- How can you reduce the amount of force needed to accelerate an object?

- When might it be desirable to reduce mass to increase acceleration?

- How might a bicycle racer reduce the mass of her bicycle in order to increase acceleration?

- How does a bicycle racer increase the force he exerts on the pedals of the bike?

Dynamics

APPLYING THE SECOND LAW

Newton's second law of motion can be used to calculate the amount of force needed to accelerate a particular object or to predict an object's acceleration with a given force. This equation is very important in many areas of engineering. For example, when an engineer is trying to design a new car, he needs to decide how powerful the engine needs to be. The engine must be large enough to supply sufficient power for the car to accelerate at a reasonable rate. If the engine is too small for the mass of the car, the car will accelerate too slowly for the customer to be satisfied. If the engine is too big, it will use too much gasoline and the customer will be wasting money. Therefore, the engineer must design the engine to be just the right size.

Pretend you are the designer and complete the "Applying the Second Law of Motion" worksheet.

A minivan needs a more powerful engine than a small car.

THIRD LAW OF MOTION

Equal and opposite

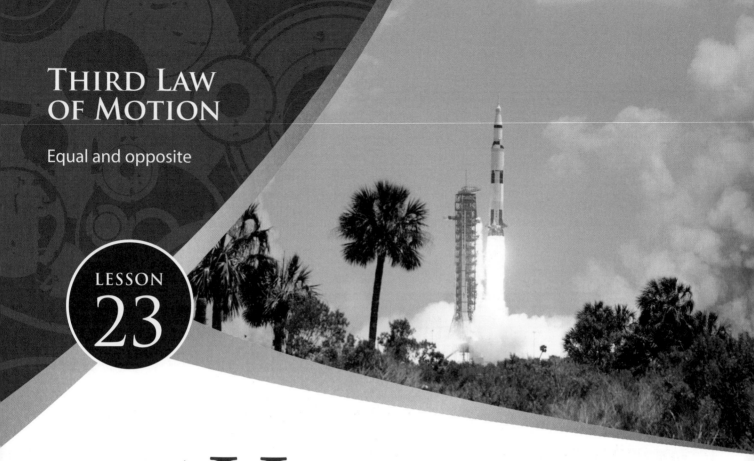

Dynamics

What is the law of action and reaction?

Words to know:

third law of motion

law of action and reaction

Have you ever seen the space shuttle launch into space, or seen a rocket shoot into the sky? Have you ever wondered what makes the rocket engine work? Newton's **third law of motion** explains how a rocket engine is able to boost the huge shuttle into space. Newton's third law of motion is often called the **law of action and reaction**. It states that "for every action there is an equal and opposite reaction." The reaction is equal in strength and opposite in direction to the original action. Inside a rocket engine, hydrogen and oxygen are ignited in a forceful explosion. The hot gases from this explosion are forced out the back of the engine. The backward force of the moving gases creates an equal force in the opposite (forward) direction, thus pushing the rocket forward.

We experience equal and opposite reactions all the time. When you are sitting in a chair, gravity is pulling down on your body so your body is exerting

FUN FACT

A squid uses Newton's third law of motion to move through the water. The sea animal squirts a jet of water out the back of its body. The equal and opposite reaction to this squirt propels the squid forward through the water.

EXPERIENCING THE THIRD LAW

Purpose: To observe Newton's third law of motion

Materials: balloon, roller skates

Activity 1—Procedure:

1. Fill a balloon with air and release it. What happens to the balloon? It goes flying across the room. Why does the balloon fly through the air?

Conclusion: The air rushing out the back is the action. The reaction is the balloon moving forward in the opposite direction. This is the same principle as the rocket engine.

Activity 2—Procedure:

1. Have two people wearing roller skates face each other. Have one person place her hands on the other's shoulders and push the other person backward. What happened to each person?

Conclusion: The person doing the pushing moves backward with the same force that she pushed on the other person. You experience this same push when you push on a wall, except the wall does not move, it pushes back against your hands.

a downward force on the chair. The chair is exerting an upward force on your body that is equal to your weight. If the chair did not push up with the same force that your body is pushing down you would fall right through the chair. Similarly, when you walk, the ground pushes up against your foot with the same force that your foot pushes down against the ground. This makes it easy to walk.

Another example of equal and opposite forces is seen when you observe a rower in a rowboat. The rower pulls backward with the oar. This is the action. The boat moves forward in the water. This is the reaction. The boat moves with a force equal to the force of the oar through the water, and the boat moves in the opposite direction of the force of the oar. This is Newton's third law of motion in action.

Look around you and try to identify as many cases of the third law as you can find. ■

Dynamics

WHAT DID WE LEARN?

- What is Newton's third law of motion?
- How can reactions be both equal and opposite?

TAKING IT FURTHER

- How does a rifle demonstrate Newton's third law of motion?
- How might you reduce the "kick" of a rifle?

AVIATION RESEARCH

Newton's third law of motion is very important in aviation. Both helicopters and airplanes use the action/reaction principle for flight. Research how helicopters and jet engines work and write a short description of how the third law of motion is used in each case.

GRAVITY

It's pulling you down

LESSON 24

Dynamics

How does gravity work?

Words to know:

law of gravitation

It has been said that what goes up must come down. What have you seen in your experiences? In general, when something goes up in the air, even if it floats for a while, it will eventually come back down to earth. Airplanes, birds, balloons, even the water in the clouds—they all eventually come back down to the ground. This is because of a force called gravity. The only things that do not come back down are items such as space probes that are sent far enough away from the earth to escape the earth's gravitational pull.

When we study how objects move, it doesn't take very long to realize that gravity is a force that cannot be ignored. Sir Isaac Newton is credited with "discovering" gravity. While he did not really discover gravity, he was the first to recognize gravity as a universal force—that is, a force that works throughout the universe. Newton studied this force and after much research and testing, he devised the law of gravitation and was able to explain the gravitational pull mathematically. The **law of gravitation** states: "Any two bodies attract each other with a force proportional to the product of their masses and inversely proportional to the square of the distance between them."

This law may sound a little confusing, so let's look at it piece by piece. The first part of this law says that any two bodies attract each other. This means that all objects exert a gravitational pull. However, the second part says that this force is proportional to their masses. This means that the more massive something is the more gravitational force it exerts.

The mass of the earth is much, much greater than anything on the earth; therefore, it exerts a much stronger pull than any other object on earth. Gravity is a very weak force, so unless an object is extremely large, such as a moon or a planet, we cannot feel the gravity it exerts.

PLAYING WITH GRAVITY

Although Newton was the first to mathematically describe gravitational forces, he was not the first to recognize the pull of gravity on objects. Galileo, who died the same year that Newton was born, did many experiments with gravity to try to understand the force that causes objects to fall.

Until Galileo began his experiments, most scientists believed that the heavier an object was, the faster it would fall. However, Galileo reasoned that this was not true, that all objects should fall at the same rate. Tradition has it that he tested his theory by dropping items from the leaning tower of Pisa and measuring how long it took for them to hit the ground. He showed that objects fall at the same rate regardless of their masses. You can show this to be true by trying a few experiments yourself.

Purpose: To understand how mass affects gravitational pull

Materials: heavy book, pen, piece of paper

Procedure:

1. Hold a heavy book and a pen waist high. Which is more massive, the book or the pen?

2. Release both objects at the same time and note when they hit the floor. They should hit the floor at about the same time. Even though the book has more mass, it falls at the same rate as the pen.

3. Hold the book and a piece of paper waist high. Predict which object will hit the floor first.

4. Drop both objects. Did they hit the floor at the same time? No, the paper fell more slowly than the book. Was this because the paper is lighter? Not really. The paper was slowed down by the resistance of the air. Air molecules are pushing against both the book and paper as they fall.

However, because the book has more inertia the air resistance has less effect on the book than on the paper. This is more a function of the shape of the paper than of its mass.

5. Place the sheet of paper on top of the book and drop them together. Did they fall at the same rate? Yes, because the book blocked the air molecules from reaching the falling paper, thus they could fall at the same rate.

6. Crumple up the paper into a small ball. Now drop the book and the paper side by side. Did they both hit the floor at the same time? They should, because the air resistance is minimal against the paper when it is in a small ball. The paper ball falls faster than the sheet of paper even though the mass of the paper is unchanged.

Dynamics

The sun is much larger than the earth so it has a stronger gravitational pull, but its gravitational pull does not affect objects on the earth very much because the sun is too far away to have a significant effect. This brings us to the third part of the law of gravitation, which says that the gravitational force becomes less the farther away the objects are from each other. We are very close to the earth so we are affected by its gravitational pull. But we are far away from the sun and the other planets and stars so their gravity does not have a significant effect on us.

Gravity plays a very important role in every motion on earth. It also plays a very important role in the motion of the universe. The moon orbits the earth and the earth revolves around the sun because of gravity. The gravitational pull of the moon pulls the waters of the oceans and causes the tides to move in and out. God designed the universe to work precisely the way it does and He uses gravity to keep it all moving. ■

WHAT DID WE LEARN?

- What is gravity?
- What two factors affect the strength of gravitational pull?
- Who defined the laws of motion and the law of gravitation?

TAKING IT FURTHER

- Why can't you feel gravitational pull from other people?
- Since the earth is slightly flattened at the poles, do people at the North Pole experience more, less, or the same gravitational pull as people at the equator?
- Do people in tall skyscrapers experience more or less gravity than people on the ground?
- What is the strength of the gravitational pull on your body?
- Would the strength of the gravitational pull be more or less if you were on the moon? Why?

FUN FACT

During the Apollo 15 mission to the moon, astronaut David R. Scott performed a very interesting experiment. He dropped a hammer and a falcon feather at the same time. On earth the hammer would fall more quickly than the feather because air resistance would slow down the feather. However, on the moon there is no atmosphere so both items fell to the ground in 1.33 seconds.

David R. Scott with hammer and feather

GRAVITATIONAL FORCE

The law of gravitation says that the gravitational force between objects is proportional to the product of their masses and inversely proportional to the square of the distance between them. This can be expressed by the following equation:

$$F = G \frac{m_1 m_2}{d^2}$$

F represents the gravitational force, G is the gravitational constant, which is a very small number that accounts for the units of gravity, m_1 and m_2 are the masses of the two objects, and d is the distance between the objects, as measured from their centers.

From this equation we can see that if we replace one object with an object that is twice as massive, the gravitational force is twice as much. Or if we replace it with an object that is half as massive, then the gravitational force is half as much. This is what it means when the law says that the force is proportional to the mass.

Since distance is on the bottom of the equation we see that as distance increases the force decreases. This is what it means when the law says that the force is inversely proportional to distance. Also, the distance is a square function, so if the distance between the objects is doubled, the force decreases by 2 squared or 4 times. If the distance between the objects is three times farther apart, the force decreases by 9 times.

To better understand how the law of gravitation works, complete the "Gravitational Force" worksheet.

The Leaning Tower of Pisa

FALLING BODIES

Are you falling?

Dynamics

How do objects fall through the air?

Words to know:

terminal velocity

When Galileo began testing his ideas, he was doing something that very few scientists had done in nearly 2,000 years—experiments. Most scientists from the time of Aristotle until Galileo believed in thinking about a subject and trying to explain it logically, but they did not perform experiments to verify that what they thought to be true was actually correct. Galileo took a different approach and decided to do experiments and draw conclusions from what he observed. Sir Francis Bacon lived in England at the same time as Galileo and also supported the idea of drawing conclusions from experimental data. In fact, Bacon is often credited with "inventing" the scientific method. Therefore, Galileo and Bacon are considered the fathers of modern experimental science.

Sir Francis Bacon

Some of the most important experiments that Galileo did were his falling body experiments. Before he did his experiments, he thought about the problem and proposed a solution; however, he did not stop there. Galileo designed experiments to test his ideas, and then performed the experiments to see if he was right. This is the basis of today's scientific method. When Galileo thought about falling bodies, he considered Aristotle's idea that a heavy object falls more quickly than a lighter object. He was not sure this was true so he did a thought experiment first.

Galileo

Galileo envisioned two equal weights being dropped from a height at the same time, knowing they would fall together and hit the ground at the same time.

THE GREAT EGG DROP

Because falling bodies accelerate, many ways have been invented to slow them down. For example, a parachute is designed to catch as much air resistance as possible to slow a person who is falling through the air.

Use your imagination and design a container that will protect an egg from the effects of gravity. Your container can be anything you like as long as an adult approves. Build your container and place a raw egg inside of it. Drop it from a height of

at least 10 feet and see if the egg survives the fall. If you are successful, try dropping it from a greater height. Does the height make a difference? Why or why not?

He then pictured the weights being tied together by a very light chain and being dropped. The weights would still fall together. He then pictured making the chain shorter and shorter until the weights were touching. This essentially made the two weights into one weight with twice the mass, but he realized that the heavier weight would still fall at the same rate as the two smaller weights. This caused him to think that all objects would fall at the same rate if there were no air resistance. He tested this theory and found it to be correct.

Galileo also found that falling objects do not fall at a constant speed. Objects speed up the longer they fall, and he found that they speed up at a uniform rate. The rate at which objects speed up is the same for all objects on earth. This rate is called acceleration due to gravity and this is often symbolized by the lowercase letter g. Galileo did not have the instruments to accurately measure this acceleration, but later scientists were able to determine that the acceleration due to gravity on earth is 32.2 feet per second^2 (9.8 m/s^2). This means that each second the velocity of a falling object is increasing by 32.2 feet per second. So if you drop an object off of a high cliff after one second it would be traveling at 32.2 feet per second. After 2 seconds it would be traveling 64.4 feet per second and so on. The acceleration due to gravity would be different on other planets with different masses because their gravitational pulls would be different.

WHAT DID WE LEARN?

- What did Galileo discover about the speed and acceleration of falling bodies?
- What is terminal velocity?
- Why do falling objects have a terminal velocity?

TAKING IT FURTHER

- How was Galileo's approach to science different from other scientists?
- Why is it important to test your scientific theories?
- Can all theories be tested?
- Which will hit the ground first, a bullet fired from a gun, or a bullet dropped from the height of the gun?

Objects dropped from great heights, such as from an airplane, can reach very high speeds. However, there is a limit to how fast an object can fall. Air molecules are pushing up on objects as they are falling down. Eventually the amount of air resistance is enough to prevent the object from accelerating any more. This maximum speed of a falling object is called terminal velocity. On earth, the terminal velocity of a person falling through the air is about 177 feet per second (54 m/s), which is about 120 miles per hour (193 km/h). ■

FALLING BALLS

It seems logical to think that heavier objects should fall faster than lighter objects; however, experimentation shows that this is not true. So how can falling bodies defy logic? They don't if you understand all of the laws of motion. First, consider the law of gravitation. Assume you drop a 1 pound ball and a 10 pound ball from the top of a building. What force does gravity exert on each of them? Recall the equation for the force of gravity:

$$F = G \, \frac{m_1 \, m_2}{d^2}$$

Since the gravitational constant (G), the distance the balls travel (d), and the mass of the earth (m_1) are the same for each ball, the only difference in the force is due to the mass of each ball (m_2). Thus, the force of gravity for the 10 pound ball is 10 times greater than the force of gravity for the 1 pound ball.

But we can't stop with the gravity. We must also look at the first and second laws of motion. The first law says that inertia causes an object to resist changing its speed. The 10 pound ball has more inertia than the 1 pound ball. The second law says that:

$$F = ma$$

To find the acceleration that the ball is experiencing we can rewrite this equation as:

$$a = F/m$$

The force on the 10 pound ball is 10 times greater than the force on the 1 pound ball, but the mass of the 10 pound ball is also 10 times greater than the mass of the 1 pound ball, so the acceleration each ball experiences is the same. The heavier ball has more inertia and resists the force of gravity the same amount as the increase in the force, so the balls fall at the same rate.

Purpose: To see if mass affects how fast things fall

Materials: shoe box lid, thin cardboard, tape, bucket or cup, several different-sized balls (for example, a marble, golf ball, and tennis ball)

Procedure:

1. First, create a chute to roll the balls down. Cut a shoebox lid into two unequal pieces.

2. Cut a half circle out of each piece as shown here.

3. Cut a strip of thin cardboard or heavy paper 10 inches long and wide enough to fit inside the circles.

4. Tape the cardboard in place to make a chute and place your chute on a large box or a table.

5. Place a bucket or cup on the floor to catch the balls as they roll down the chute. Try to predict where each ball will land and move the bucket to the location you expect the ball to fall, and then roll each of the balls down the chute.

Questions:

Which ball do you expect to fly the farthest? Why? Test your hypothesis. Were you right?

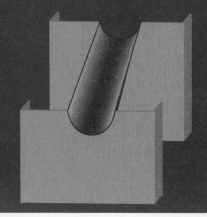

Dynamics

CENTER OF MASS

What is in the middle?

LESSON 26

Why is understanding center of mass important?

Words to know:

center of mass

center of gravity

Have you ever seen a human balancing act where several people stand on each other to form a human pyramid? Or perhaps you have seen someone balancing on the side of a bicycle as it races in a circle? How can these people balance at such odd angles without tumbling to the ground? They can do it because they have learned about center of mass, which is also called the center of gravity.

As you know, gravity pulls down on everything on earth. But gravity acts on the point where the mass of each object seems to be concentrated. With a sphere, such as the earth, the center of mass is the center of the sphere. So the earth attracts everything toward its center. This is why objects all over the world are attracted to the earth and there is not an up and down or top and bottom to our planet.

With the human balancing act, the people must arrange their bodies in such a way that their combined center of mass is directly above the feet of the lowest person. If their center of mass is too far to one side, gravity will pull them over.

When loading a weight on a wagon or cart, you must be sure that the center of mass is over the area between the wheels. If the center of mass is to the side of the base, the load will become unstable and fall over.

UNDERSTANDING CENTER OF MASS

How the mass of an object is arranged around the center of mass determines how the mass will move. This is especially important when objects are rotating around their centers of mass.

Purpose: To understand center of mass

Materials: marble, two canning jar rings, roll of masking tape, cardboard or wood, books

Procedure:

1. Use a small amount of tape to tape the two rings' top sides together. You now have three objects with about the same mass, depending on how much tape is on your roll of tape.

    Where is the center of mass for each object? The center of mass for the marble is in the center of the marble. The center of mass for the rings and for the roll of tape is in the center of them even though there is no mass at that point. This center is the point that gravity is pulling down on.

2. Now, use a ruler and measure the distance from the center to the edge of each object.

    Which object has the mass closest to the center? Which object has the mass farthest from the center?

3. Make a ramp using a piece of cardboard or wood and a stack of books.

4. Set each object at the top of the ramp and let them all roll down at the same time. Which object rolled down the ramp the fastest?

Conclusion: The marble will roll faster. With the mass closer to the center of gravity, it is able to rotate more quickly than the other objects.

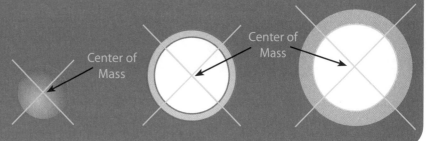

Center of Mass

Center of Mass

When a baby is first learning to walk, he often falls down because he hasn't learned to keep his balance by keeping his center of mass above his feet. You don't give this a second thought because your brain has learned to keep your center of mass in balance. Learning to ride a bicycle is a similar experience. You must learn to keep your center of mass in the center of the bike above the pedals. ■

WHAT DID WE LEARN?

- What is the center of mass of an object?
- What is another name for center of mass?

TAKING IT FURTHER

- Is the center of gravity always in the center of an object?
- What would the effect be of placing a piece of clay inside a ball against one side?

Dynamics

FINDING CENTER OF MASS

Finding the center of mass or the center of gravity for uniform objects such as spheres or rings is relatively easy. However, most objects are not uniform so it is more difficult to find the center of mass for most objects.

Purpose: To locate the center of mass for irregularly shaped objects

Materials: tag board, scissors, hole punch, push pin, pencil, string, ruler

Procedure:

1. Draw a squiggly irregular shape on a piece of tag board or thin cardboard.

2. Cut out your shape.

Steps 1 & 2

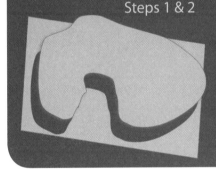

3. Punch four holes equally spaced around the edge of the shape.

4. Using one of these holes, hang up the cardboard with a push pin or tack.

5. Tie a weight such as a pencil or other small object to one end of a string and tie the other end of the string to the tack, allowing the weight to pull the string straight down.

6. Use a ruler to draw a line showing where the string hangs down.

Steps 3 & 6

7. Repeat steps 4–6 for each of the four holes.

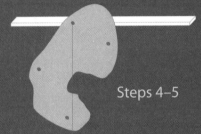

Steps 4–5

Conclusion: When you are done you will have a point where all four lines cross. This is the center of mass for your piece of cardboard. This is the point at which gravity is pulling down on your shape. Try balancing the shape on your finger (or the tip of a pencil) by placing your finger on the point where the lines cross.

Final step

FUN FACT

Because your center of mass is above your waist, it is difficult to do some things that seem like they should be simple. Stand with your back and heels against a wall. Try to bend over and touch your toes without bending your legs. Even if you can touch your toes while standing in the middle of a room, you can't do it against the wall because your center of mass is pulling you over. Turn around and stand about 12 inches from the wall. Lean forward and place your forehead against the wall. Put your arms to your side and keep your body straight. Now try to stand up straight. Again, you can't do it because your center of mass is not above your feet.

UNIT 5

CIRCULAR & PERIODIC MOTION

◊ **Describe** how a satellite orbiting the earth is an example of angular momentum.

◊ **Illustrate** periodic motion using a pendulum as a model.

KEY CONCEPTS

UNIT LESSONS

27 Circular Motion • 91
28 Motion of the Planets • 94
29 Periodic Motion • 99
30 Pendulums • 102

CIRCULAR MOTION

Spinning around

LESSON
27

How do we describe circular motion?

Words to know:

ballistics

centripetal force

angular momentum

Challenge words:

centrifugal force

When a force is applied to an object it causes that object to move in a straight line in the direction of the force. This is easy to understand when you think about balls on a pool table (see photo at top of page 72). When you hit the cue ball with the pool cue, the ball moves forward in a straight line until it hits another ball. The second ball will move in a straight line from the force of the cue ball. However, when you think about how things move someplace other than on a flat surface like the pool table, you realize that objects don't always move in straight lines. Does this mean that they are not following Newton's laws of motion? No, it means that there is more than one force affecting the motion of the object.

For example, when you throw a ball at a target you are applying a force in a horizontal direction. The ball begins to move in the horizontal direction, but as it goes through the air it begins to fall, so it actually moves in an arc through the air. If you toss the ball up it will still move in an arc. This is because gravity is pulling down on the ball as it is moving up or forward. The study of objects moving through the air is called ballistics. Other objects that move in arcs include bullets, cannon balls, and artillery shells.

Other objects move in circles. Objects moving in circles are said to have circular motion. An object moving in a circle is constantly experiencing a force that is changing its direction. Think about a ball on a string. If you twirl the string above your head the ball will move in a circle around you. The ball is trying to move in a straight line, but your continuous tug on the string is constantly changing its direction, causing it to move in a circle. The force applied to an object that causes it to move in a circle is called centripetal force. Centripetal means toward the center, so it is a force making the object move

OBSERVING CIRCULAR MOTION

Purpose: To observe circular motion

Materials: Styrofoam or paper cup, hole punch, string, scissors

Procedure:

1. Punch two holes on opposite sides near the top of a Styrofoam or paper cup.

2. Cut a 30-inch long piece of string and tie one end of the string through one hole and the other end of the string through the other hole.

3. Fill the cup half full of water.

4. Take the cup outside and while holding on to the center of the string, swing the cup in a circle so that the cup goes upside down.

Conclusion: The water will not come out of the cup because of the angular momentum of the water forcing it toward the bottom of the cup, even when it is upside down.

PLAYING WITH A GYROSCOPE

If you have a gyroscope, you can observe the effects of angular momentum. The angular momentum of the spinning wheels in a gyroscope allows it to balance in nearly any position. Spin the gyro and try to balance it on your finger. Try to balance it on the tip of a pencil. You might even be able to turn it on its side and hold it with a piece of string around one end. Gyroscopes are important parts of instruments in airplanes, rockets, and space probes.

toward the center of the circle. If the force is removed—if you let go of the string, for example—what will happen to the ball? Recall your test in lesson 1. It will go flying off in a straight line away from you and move in an arc until it hits the ground (unless it hits a window first!).

Objects don't have to be pulled toward the center to move in a circle. Sometimes the centripetal force is a push toward the center. Consider a roller coaster whose cars sit on the track with a loop in it. The cars of the roller coaster gain speed going down a hill, then as they head up another hill they want to keep going in a straight line. But the track bends, applying a force to the bottom of the cars pushing them toward the center and making them go in a circle. The passengers do not fall out of the car however, because according to the third law of motion, the passengers are pushing out with the same force that the car is pushing in on them and this keeps them in their seats.

Objects moving in a circle have momentum just like objects moving in a straight line. Because the object moves through the angles of a circle, this momentum is called **angular momentum**. Angular momentum explains why a spinning ice skater speeds up when she pulls in her arms. In straight-line movement, momentum is a function of mass and velocity. But in angular momentum, the momentum is a function of the radius of the circle in addition to the mass and the velocity. A figure skater begins her spin with her arms out wide. This gives the circle of the spin a large radius. We know that momentum must be conserved, so as she draws in her arms the radius of the circle becomes smaller, so either her mass or her velocity must go up to conserve momentum. Obviously, her mass cannot go up during the spin, so her velocity must increase and she begins spinning faster. This is just like the marble experiment from the previous lesson. The marble rolled faster than the other objects because its radius was smaller. ■

WHAT DID WE LEARN?

- What causes an object flying through the air to move in an arc?
- What causes an object to move in a circular path?
- What is the name of the force that causes an object to move in a circle?

TAKING IT FURTHER

- What groups of people might need to understand ballistics?
- If you shoot a jet of water into the air, what shape would you expect the water to make and why?

CENTRIFUGAL FORCE

In the previous experiment, the centripetal (inward) force caused the cup and water to move in a circle. People often refer to another force, an outward force, called centrifugal force. Centrifugal means "away from the center."

Centrifugal force is actually a fictitious force. This can be seen by considering a passenger riding in a car. When a car swerves around a corner, the passenger's body seems to move towards the outer edge of the car. In the reference frame of the people in the car, it looks as if a force is pushing the passenger away from the center of the bend. But there is not an actual force exerted by any other object on the passenger.

Centrifugal force is felt by children on a merry-go-round. It is also used in many applications today. One application is a centrifuge. A

centrifuge is a device that spins liquids. One liquid that is sent through a centrifuge is unseparated milk. As the liquid spins, the heavier milk molecules have more momentum than the lighter cream molecules and move to the outside of the centrifuge, while the cream molecules stay in the center. Thus, the cream is separated from the milk. This produces skim milk and provides cream for many uses. A centrifuge is also used in medicine to separate heavy red blood cells from lighter plasma.

Centrifugal force is also used in seed and fertilizer spreaders. As the seed or fertilizer particles flow down onto a spinning platform they are accelerated and gain angular momentum. This momentum gives them centrifugal force causing them to move away from the center of the spinning

platform and out onto the ground.

Can you think of an instance in the Bible where these forces played an important role? Think about the story of David and Goliath. David used a rock from a sling to kill the giant. The rock was placed in the sling. The sling was spun around David's head and the rock was accelerated. When one end of the sling was released, the centripetal force that was forcing the stone in a circle was removed and the forward momentum of the rock carried it in a straight line to the giant's forehead.

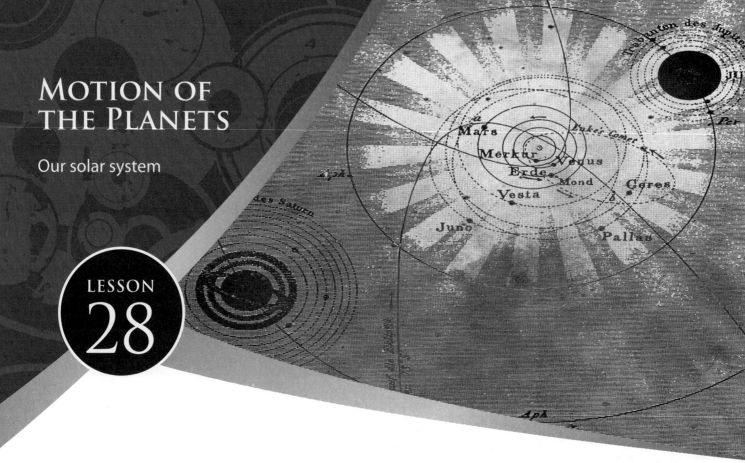

MOTION OF THE PLANETS

Our solar system

How do the planets follow the laws of motion?

Periodic Motion

Sir Isaac Newton's law of gravitation is more correctly called the law of universal gravitation because Newton proved that the force of gravity that we experience on earth is the same force that is at work throughout the universe. As we mentioned before, the moon orbits the earth because of the force of gravity. At creation, the moon was given a forward momentum so it would want to move in a straight line; however, the gravitational pull of the earth continually pulls the moon toward it, causing the moon to move in a nearly circular pattern around the earth. The moon is actually continuously falling toward the earth, but its forward momentum continually moves it away from the earth by the same amount.

Satellites and space shuttles also experience this same motion. As a satellite is placed in orbit around the earth, it is given a forward momentum that is equal to the gravitational force exerted by the earth so that it stays a constant distance from the earth. Similarly, all of the planets in our solar system are falling toward the sun because of the sun's gravitational pull, but they are moving forward because of their momentum, thus causing them to orbit the sun.

Halley's comet last appeared in 1986.

Edmond Halley

OBSERVING CENTRIPETAL FORCES

Purpose: To observe centripetal forces

Materials: string, tennis ball

Procedure:

Note: This activity should be done outside.

1. Tie a three-foot long string to a tennis ball.

2. Hold the string 15 inches from the ball and twirl the ball around your head. The force you are exerting on the string is the centripetal force that is keeping the ball orbiting around you instead of flying away. The ball represents a planet and you represent the sun. You are exerting a force on the ball representing the gravitational force of the sun.

3. Stop swinging the ball and move your hand to a spot on the string that is 25 inches from the ball.

4. Again, swing the ball around your head. Try to make the ball spin more slowly than you did before. How does the force you used compare with the force you used when the string was shorter? It should be less.

Conclusion: This demonstrates why planets that are farther away from the sun orbit at a slower speed—the sun exerts less gravitational force on them.

A scientist named Johannes Kepler, who lived at about the same time as Galileo, described the movements of the planets as ellipses, which are stretched-out circles. He also showed that planets farther from the sun move in slower orbits than those closer to the sun. Newton's law of universal gravitation was able to explain what Kepler observed. Gravity decreases as objects get farther apart. So the sun exerts less gravitational force on the planets that are farther away than it does on the closer planets. With less gravitational or centripetal force, the planet needs less forward momentum to stay in orbit so it moves more slowly around the sun.

Other objects in space also experience this same motion. Once Newton was able to mathematically explain how the gravitational forces keep planets and moons in orbit, he was able to show that comets move through the solar system in elliptical orbits as well. Edmond Halley used Newton's equations to predict that a comet that had appeared in 1531, 1607, and 1682 would appear again in 1758. Halley died in 1742, but when the comet returned in 1758 as he had predicted, the comet was named Halley's Comet in his honor. Halley's Comet continues to be seen from earth every 75–76 years.

Newton's laws have proven to be so accurate that astronomers were able to discover a planet by observing the orbits of the known planets. Scientists noticed that Uranus's orbit had a slight wobble. They predicted that this was caused by the gravitational pull of another, at that time unknown, planet. Two astronomers calculated where the planet would have to be in order to cause the wobble, and in 1846 Neptune was discovered right where they predicted it would have to be. Although Newton defined the law of universal gravitation, he did not invent gravity or the law. God set all of the laws of motion in place when He created the universe. ∎

WHAT DID WE LEARN?

- Why is Newton's law called the universal law of gravitation?
- How does gravity affect the motion of the planets in our solar system?
- What is the shape of a planet's orbit?

TAKING IT FURTHER

- Which objects in space are affected by the sun's gravity?
- Do planets revolve around the sun at a constant speed?

SPACE SHUTTLE & LAWS OF MOTION

Consider the launch and orbit of the space shuttle. All three of Newton's laws of motion as well as his law of gravitation play very important roles. Describe which law or laws are being demonstrated by the space shuttle as you complete the "Space Shuttle and the Laws of Motion" worksheet.

FUN FACT

Following is a chart showing the average distance each planet is from the sun and the length of time it takes for that planet to revolve around the sun. This chart shows that the farther away a planet is, the slower it moves around the sun, and thus the longer it takes to make a complete revolution.

Planet	Average distance from sun (in millions)	Revolution around sun
Mercury	36 miles (58 km)	88 days
Venus	67 miles (108 km)	224.7 days
Earth	93 miles (150 km)	365.26 days (1 year)
Mars	143 miles (230 km)	628 days
Jupiter	483 miles (778 km)	11.86 years
Saturn	887 miles (1427 km)	29.46 years
Uranus	1,783 miles (2870 km)	84 years
Neptune	2,794 miles (4497 km)	164.8 years

Periodic Motion

JOHANNES KEPLER

1571–1630

Johannes Kepler is the mathematician/ astronomer that gave us the first three laws of planetary motion, which are very important in the understanding of the wonderful universe that God made for us. But who was he and what other things did he do for us?

Johannes was the oldest child in a poor family. He was born in a small town called Weil der Stadt in an area that is now part of Southwestern Germany. His father was a mercenary soldier who died in a war in the Netherlands when Johannes was only five. His mother was the daughter of an innkeeper, and after her husband died she and the children moved back in with her father at the inn.

Kepler's intelligence was obvious at a very young age, and upon completion of his elementary education he was enrolled at the University of Tubingen, a Lutheran Orthodox school. Kepler had a very deep faith in God throughout his life and he felt it was his duty as a Christian to understand the works of God. Kepler was convinced that God had made the universe according to a mathematical plan, and man, being made in the image of God, was clearly capable of understanding the universe that God had created. In Kepler's writings he thanked God repeatedly for giving him

insights into His creation.

While at the University, Kepler studied mathematics along with Greek and Hebrew. He was an outstanding student and was part of a special math class where he learned about the new teachings on the Copernican model of the solar system, where the sun and not the earth is the center of the solar system. Kepler accepted this new information instantly as being true. Because of this acceptance, and some of his other beliefs about God, Kepler was able to sign the Augsburg confession for Lutheranism, but was not able to sign the Formula of Concord, which in part said the earth was the center of the universe. Because he refused to sign this document, Kepler was excluded from the sacrament in the Lutheran church.

Kepler also refused to convert to Catholicism, the only other Christian church in the area at the time. This made life difficult for him and his family, as he had to move several times to find kings who allowed more religious freedom. This did little to slow down his work, however, and he was still able to make several very import scientific discoveries.

Kepler was the first to correctly explain planetary motion and give us the laws that describe it. He later was the first to investigate the formation of pictures with a small-hole (pin-hole) camera and in doing so came up with the correct explanation of how refraction works. He also explained how to formulate eyeglasses for nearsightedness and farsightedness. And he explained that God gave us two eyes for depth perception.

Even though Kepler did not invent the telescope, he was the first to explain how it worked. He also derived the birth year of Christ that is now almost universally accepted and he was the first to suggest that the sun rotates on its own axis. He was the one who explained that the ocean tides are caused by the moon and he coined the word "satellite" (attendant) for our moon and the other moons in our solar system.

As you think about all Johannes Kepler did, remember that he lived the same time as William Shakespeare (1564–1616) and Galileo (1564–1642). The King James Version of the Bible was published during his lifetime (1611) and the Pilgrims landed at Plymouth (1620) ten years before he died. It was an exciting time in history as man's understanding of the world was changing.

For more on Kepler's life and discoveries, see www.answersingenesis.org/go/kepler.

PERIODIC MOTION

Can you keep time?

What is periodic motion?

Words to know:

periodic motion

pendulum

oscillation

Challenge words:

cycle

period

frequency

mean position

amplitude

damping

What do you think of when you hear the phrase, "a period of time"? Do you think of a second or a minute? Maybe you think of a week or a year. These are all periods of time. When something happens periodically, that means that it happens once during a certain period of time. For example, a newspaper is called a periodical because it is printed once during a specific period of time—every day or every week.

When we talk about **periodic motion** (also called *harmonic motion*), we are talking about a movement that happens over and over again at a regular interval. Circular motion is one type of periodic motion. Something moving in a circle reaches the same location over and over again during the same period of time. If a disk is spinning at 100 revolutions per minute, a particular point on the disk passes through the same location 100 times each minute. The periodic motion of the earth causes it to revolve around the sun and move through the same location in space once each year—once in approximately 365¼ days. This is one type of periodic motion.

Another type of periodic motion is the motion of a spring. A spring has a natural position that it wants to be in. If the spring is stretched or compressed out of that position it is storing potential energy. When the force stretching or compressing the spring is removed, the spring will move back and forth until it reaches equilibrium—its natural state. This is periodic motion.

If a spring is hung vertically and a weight is placed on one end, gravity will pull down on the weight. The spring will pull up with the same force that gravity is pulling down because of Newton's third law. When you stretch the spring by pulling down on the weight and then release it, the weight will

SPRING ACTION

Purpose: To observe periodic motion with a metal spring toy

Materials: metal spring toy (such as a Slinky®), set of stairs

Procedure:

1. Hold one end of the Slinky® so that it hangs down vertically.

2. Have someone pull down on the other end of the Slinky® and then release it. Watch as it moves up and down. These periodic movements are called oscillations. The Slinky® oscillates up and down.

3. If you have stairs, set the Slinky® at the edge of the top stair.

4. Stretch the top of the Slinky® down until it reaches the edge of the next step.

5. Release the Slinky® and watch it "walk" down the stairs. It might take a few tries to get it just right. Why does the Slinky® do this?

Conclusion: The Slinky® is a big spring. It wants to return to its equilibrium position so it contracts after you stretch it out. This gives the spring forward momentum. As

the spring leaves the top step, its forward momentum pulls it forward and gravity pulls it down so the top moves in an arc, taking it down another step. This continues until the spring reaches the bottom step.

move up and down. If you measure how long it takes the weight to move up and back down, you will find that the length of time is the same regardless of how far you stretch the spring. How can this be? Shouldn't it take longer for the weight to move through a longer distance? Not if it is moving faster. Newton's second law requires that the weight move faster because of the additional force on the mass.

Another important kind of periodic motion occurs with a pendulum. A **pendulum** is a weight suspended from a string, chain, or pole. When the weight is lifted to the side and then released, it moves back and forth in an arc. This periodic motion has some very interesting properties, one of which is that the period of the pendulum is constant regardless of the size of the arc.

This constant rate of periodic motion in spring/mass combinations and in pendulums is very important in many modern instruments. Perhaps the most important invention to use periodic motion is the clock. You will learn more about pendulums and clocks in the next lesson. ■

WHAT DID WE LEARN?

- What is periodic motion?
- Give three examples of periodic motion.
- What is one invention that uses the periodic motion of springs and pendulums?

TAKING IT FURTHER

- Why do the oscillations of a spring or pendulum eventually stop?

KEY TERMS

It is important to know the terminology associated with periodic motion. Take a few minutes and memorize the definitions of each of the following terms.

Cycle—One complete movement, such as up and down of a spring or one complete revolution

Oscillation—Movement between two extremes (Oscillation is the changing of potential energy into kinetic energy and back again. One oscillation = one cycle)

Period—The time for one complete cycle

Frequency—The number of cycles in 1 second (The units for frequency are hertz.)

Mean Position—The position about which the oscillation occurs

Amplitude—The amount an object moves in each direction around the mean position

Damping—The process causing the oscillations to die down (generally due to friction)

FUN FACT

Leon Foucault used the periodic motion of a giant pendulum to demonstrate the rotation of the earth. In 1851 he suspended a heavy weight from the domed ceiling of the Pantheon in Paris. He set the pendulum in motion above a line indicating the direction the pendulum was swinging. Several hours later the pendulum was still swinging, however it was no longer swinging along the line. The pendulum did not change directions, the earth turned under the pendulum. See lesson 3 in *God's Design for Heaven and Earth: Our Universe* for directions on how to build your own Foucault pendulum.

Periodic Motion

Pendulums

Back and forth

What is a pendulum and how does it move?

Most people have seen a clock with a pendulum swinging back and forth. The swinging of the pendulum keeps the clock on time. But how does this work? Once again we have to look at the work of Galileo. According to tradition, Galileo was sitting in church and became interested in a chandelier that was swinging from the ceiling. He noticed that when the light was moving only a little and the swing was short, it seemed to take the same amount of time to swing back and forth as it did when the breeze made the light move in a higher arc.

Galileo did not have a stopwatch or even a clock to use to time how long each swing took, so he used the only regular thing he had, his pulse. He timed how long each swing took and concluded that the length of time for each swing was not affected by the size of the arc. This surprised him, so he determined to do more testing.

As he experimented with pendulums, Galileo found that his initial observations were correct. The length of time for one complete swing did not depend on how big the swing was. Next, he tried using different masses at the end of the string. Again, he found that the time for one complete swing did not change even when the mass at the end of the string was changed. Finally, he tried making the string longer and shorter. Here is where he noticed a big difference. The longer the string, the slower the swing of the pendulum.

These were incredibly important discoveries. The fact that the time, or period, of a swinging pendulum does not change even as the size of the swing changes means that people now had a way of marking a specific time period. Galileo eventually worked out an equation that allowed him to accurately determine the period for any given pendulum. This was a very important discovery because if

GALILEO'S PENDULUM EXPERIMENTS

Repeat Galileo's experiments by making and testing your own pendulum. Record your observations on the "Pendulum Data Sheet."

you know that your pendulum always takes a set period of time to complete a swing, you can now use that pendulum to run a clock.

Prior to this discovery, many different types of clocks existed, but none was very accurate or easy to read. Shortly after Galileo's discoveries, a Dutch scientist named Christian Huygens developed the first practical pendulum clock. Of course, the pendulum alone was not enough for a clock, but the pendulum was used to drive a series of gears that in turn moved the hands of the clock. Later, Huygens developed a clock that used the oscillations of a spring, which obeys the same principles as a pendulum, to develop a smaller clock that could be used as a watch. Although many watches and clocks still use pendulums and springs, many time pieces now use vibrating crystals to regulate the time. ■

WHAT DID WE LEARN?

- What is a pendulum?
- Describe how the height from which the mass is dropped affects the period of a pendulum.
- Describe how the mass of the pendulum affects its period.
- Describe how the length of the pendulum affects its period.

TAKING IT FURTHER

- How does what we learned about falling bodies relate to the period of pendulums?

MAPPING THE EARTH

Gravity is the force that keeps a pendulum swinging back and forth. As you have just seen in the previous experiments, if the length of a pendulum is not changed, the period will not change. This is true as long as the force of gravity does not change. Using this knowledge, describe how a pendulum could be used to map the shape of the earth. Remember that gravity is a function of distance from the center of the earth.

CHRISTIAN HUYGENS

1629–1695

Have you ever wanted to do one thing but in order to get it done right you had to do something else first? In a way, this was Christian Huygens's problem when he wanted to study the planets—he had to build a better clock first. Christian Huygens was born to an important Dutch family in the Hague, Netherlands where he was tutored at home. He studied law and mathematics at the University of Leiden from 1645–1649, and after graduation he toured with a diplomatic team.

Huygens was an accomplished mathematician, but he was very interested in astronomy. He devised a better way of grinding and polishing lenses to make a better telescope. Using his new telescope, he discovered that Saturn's "ears," as Galileo described them, were actually rings made of rocks. He later found that Venus was covered with a cloud and that Mars had a day that was about 24 hours long.

Much of his work in astronomy required an accurate clock. At that time, the best clocks were only accurate to about 10 minutes a day. So Christian decided to build a better clock. He made a pendulum clock which was 10 times more accurate than other clocks. His new clock only had an error of 1 minute per day. Later he was able to build a clock that was only off by 10 seconds a day. He understood that an accurate clock was also important to ships in navigation, so he developed the cycloidal pendulum clock, which was used to accurately determine longitude for ship navigation.

In 1661 Huygens visited London's new Royal Society, which was made up of top scientists, and in 1663 he was elected to the Society. In 1666 he accepted an invitation to become part of the French Royal Academy of Science, and soon he assumed leadership of that group.

In 1667 Christian developed the balance wheel and spring assembly so that clocks could be much smaller. A similar design is still used in some watches today. He gave the first watch of this type as a gift to Louis XIV, the king of France.

Throughout his life, Huygens worked with other top scientists and mathematicians in many areas. He was the first to propose the germ theory of disease and he performed some of the first observations of human reproductive cells. He worked with Anton Van Leeuwenhoek on the first microscope. He measured the size of planets, drew pictures of the surface of Mars, observed Titan, the largest of Saturn's moons, and provided a reasonable estimate for the distance to the nearest star. He was a firm believer that life existed on other planets. Huygens died in 1695 in the same town in which he was born.

UNIT

6

USE OF
MACHINES

◊ **Describe** how machines have been used by mankind throughout history.

◊ **Identify** and **describe** simple machines in God's design of nature.

◊ **Describe**, with examples, how simple machines are combined in complex machines.

KEY CONCEPTS

31 Machines in History • 106
32 Machines in Nature • 109
33 Modern Machines • 112
34 Using Simple Machines—Final Project • 115
35 Conclusion • 117

UNIT LESSONS

MACHINES IN HISTORY

The early examples

LESSON
31

How has man used machines in the past?

Ancient civilizations were able to build amazing structures. How were they able to do this? Did they possess the knowledge of machines that we have today? The records for many of these civilizations are sketchy, but most archaeologists agree that many of the structures that we know about were built using only simple machines. Let's look at a few famous building marvels from history.

Probably the most famous ancient structures are the great pyramids of Egypt. The pyramid of Cheops is the only one of the seven "wonders of the ancient world" remaining. These amazing structures were built by a civilization that has no record of any machines. The Great Pyramid was built sometime between 2100 and 1500 BC, after the division at Babel and before the Exodus. It contained approximately 2.3 million stone blocks, each weighing an average of 2.5 tons. It is believed that these stones were cut at a nearby quarry, and then pushed on log rollers and sledges to the pyramid site. Most people believe that the stones were then pushed or pulled up a ramp that was built winding around the structure.

Recall that rolling a heavy mass across logs greatly reduces the friction, which reduces the force needed to move the stones. Also, using a ramp, especially if it is a long ramp, reduces the force needed to move the stone blocks by increasing mechanical advantage. So using a huge workforce, estimated to be at least 20,000, the Egyptians built massive stone structures using only simple machines.

Another famous structure believed to have been built using only simple machines is Stonehenge. This circle of stones was built sometime between 2000 and 1500 BC in a location that is about 85 miles southwest of London. The outer circle of stones is 30 meters in diameter and consists of 30 pillars placed in a circle. Each pillar is made of massive stones weighing about 25 tons each. On top of the

BUILDING WITH SIMPLE MACHINES

Using toothpicks as levers and/or rollers, try to move wooden blocks in place to build a structure. You may need to use other materials to build ramps or fulcrums for your levers, but do not pick up the blocks with your hands. This will give you a tiny glimpse into the difficulties faced by ancient people when trying to build their enormous structures.

pillars, 4-ton capstones were erected. No one knows exactly how these stones were put into place or who put them there. However, there are many theories.

Most archeologists believe that the stones were moved on log rollers and sledges, just as the stones of the pyramids were moved. It is believed that for each pillar, a deep hole was dug into which the pillar was to be set. The pillar was pushed forward until about one-third of the stone was over the hole. Then it is believed that a log structure was built and levers were used to slowly lift the stone until it tipped enough to slide into the hole. This is believed to have been a very labor-intensive project that required thousands of hours and hundreds of men to accomplish.

Engineer Mark Whitby has a different idea. He had a team of 120 laborers erect an exact replica of the biggest section of Stonehenge (involving moving two 40-ton stones into position and placing a 10-ton capstone on top of them) in only five days. He used what he believes was the most likely method, involving greased planks, and having each hole precut to be an exact fit.

Who built Stonehenge is an even greater mystery than how it was built. Some people believe that Druids built it for religious and astronomical purposes. But there are no records and there is much speculation as to who moved these giant stones and why they were placed where they are. Regardless of who the builders were, we know that they used their God-given intellect and simple machines to accomplish a fantastic feat of architecture. God has given people a great deal of ingenuity, and they have used that ingenuity to accomplish many things. For more on the skill of ancient man, see www.answersingenesis.org/go/pyramids. ■

Stonehenge

Use of Machines

WHAT DID WE LEARN?

- Which machines are believed to have been used by the ancient Egyptians to build the pyramids?
- Which machines are believed to have been used by the builders of Stonehenge?

TAKING IT FURTHER

- What are some advantages of using modern machines to build structures?
- Do modern machines make it possible to build stronger, more durable, or more beautiful buildings?
- If the Egyptians had the wheel, why didn't they use wheeled carts to move the large stones?

BUILDING RESEARCH

Chose a historical building or structure and research how that building or structure was built. Be sure to find out what machines were available to that group of people and how they used those machines. Choose from the structures below, or come up with an idea of your own.

Roman aqueducts

Tower of Pisa

Acropolis

Medieval castles

Medieval cathedrals

MACHINES IN NATURE

How God designed it

What machines do we see in nature?

When God created the world and all the creatures and plants in it, He set the laws of physics in place. We not only see evidence of these laws in the way everything moves on earth, but we can also see the use of simple machines in many of the plants and animals around us. Let's look at a few examples of God's magnificent designs.

The human body is an obvious place to begin to look for great design ideas. The body is full of levers. Your neck is an example of a first-class lever. Your chin acts as the resistance, you neck is the fulcrum, and the muscles at the back of the neck are the effort. A relatively small amount of effort is needed to lift your chin.

Your foot is an example of a second-class lever. To lift up the back of the foot, effort is applied to the heel. The resistance is the weight in the center of your foot and the fulcrum is the ball of your foot.

Your forearm is a wonderful third-class lever, allowing you to pick an item up and move it a long distance, say from the table to your mouth, while moving your arm near your elbow only a short distance. In this case, the effort is applied by the muscle attached below your elbow, your elbow is the

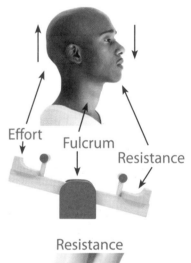

Effort   Fulcrum   Resistance

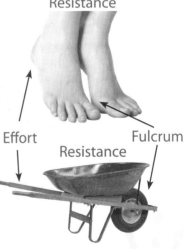

Resistance

Effort   Resistance   Fulcrum

OBSERVING NATURAL MACHINES

Muscles in your body work as levers to move your bones. Experiment by moving different parts of your body. Try to identify where the effort is being applied, where the fulcrum is, and where the resistance is. Determine which class lever each body part represents. If necessary, review the classes of levers in lesson 13.

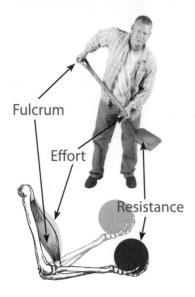

Fulcrum

Effort

Resistance

fulcrum, and the resistance is whatever you have in your hand. There are hundreds of examples of levers—basically every muscle and bone combination in your body works as a lever. This is God's design to make your body more efficient.

Plants also have some built-in levers. Leaves have the ability to turn toward the sun. This is because cells on the back of the leaves constrict. This acts like a lever, pulling the leaf to turn it. Another lever found in nature is in the Venus flytrap. The leaves of this plant can fold together to trap an unsuspecting fly. The fly does not have enough leverage from inside the leaves to push it open and free itself.

The design of plants' roots provides another example of simple machines in nature. Roots grow in such a way that the very end of the root-tip is pointed. This works as a wedge, allowing the root to push its way into the soil around it.

Root tip

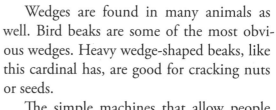

Wedges are found in many animals as well. Bird beaks are some of the most obvious wedges. Heavy wedge-shaped beaks, like this cardinal has, are good for cracking nuts or seeds.

The simple machines that allow people to accomplish work have been designed by God to make plants and animals efficient. Observe the wonder of God's creation by closely examining plants and animals. ■

WHAT DID WE LEARN?

- What types of simple machines do the muscles and bones in animals represent?
- What common simple machine is found in the shape of many animal bodies?

TAKING IT FURTHER

- What is one reason why red blood cells are disc-shaped and smooth?
- Explain why the shapes of teeth are helpful for biting into food.
- What shape does an eagle make with its body when it is diving? Why?

Use of Machines

ANIMAL WEDGES

Look at the shapes of each of the following animals. Locate which part or parts of their bodies are wedge shaped and explain how the wedge helps the animal survive. Write your ideas on the "Animal Wedges" worksheet.

Fish

Earthworm

Mosquito
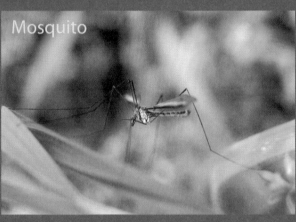

Rat

Badger

Lion

Use of Machines

MODERN MACHINES

How they work today

How do we use simple machines today?

Words to know:

efficiency

Use of Machines

Today's machines can be quite awesome. What do you think of when you think of modern machines? Do you think of huge construction equipment like bulldozers and cranes? Maybe you think of airplanes and race cars. Perhaps you think of a printing press or giant saws in a lumber mill. These are all examples of modern machines.

You have many machines in your home. You might have a blender, a toaster, a washing machine, or a hair dryer. Maybe you have a clock or a piano. These are also machines.

Machines are used every day to make it easier for people to accomplish their goals. Modern machines such as the washer and dryer have helped people do

laundry with much less time and effort than they would have to expend if they had to scrub clothes on a washboard. Computers are machines that make communication much faster and easier. It takes much less effort to type an email than to walk 10 miles to talk to your friend.

Some of the machines we use are relatively simple. From a physics point of view, a nutcracker or a broom are simple machines. A door handle and hinge are also simple machines. But many modern machines seem much more complex, and in many ways they are. However, now that you understand a little about physics, you realize that all machines are just a complex combination of simple parts.

Modern machines have been designed with levers, pulleys, gears, wheels, and wedges. These simple parts have been put together in a wide variety of ways. Shafts, chains, and belts are used to transfer power, but the basic physics of simple machines is what gives these modern machines their mechanical advantage and power.

Modern engineers use their understanding of physics to help them design more efficient machines. **Efficiency** is related to the amount of energy the machine puts out compared to the amount of energy put into the machine. You are probably familiar with this concept when it comes to your car. People often talk about the gas mileage their car

The Mars rover *Spirit* is a complicated machine.

gets. This is related to how many miles the car can travel for each gallon of gasoline that the engine uses. A more efficient car will have higher gas mileage. One car may be able to drive 18 miles on one gallon of gas while another car may be able to drive 25 miles on one gallon of gas. The second car would be more efficient than the first. Engineers are always looking for ways to make machines more efficient.

You may wonder why machines put out less energy than is put into them. This is the same question as to why perpetual motion machines are impossible. Some energy is lost due to friction and air resistance.

Engineers design machines that take advantage of the laws of physics. We have looked at some of these. The clock, for example, uses the properties of pendulums to keep accurate time. Rocket engines use equal and opposite reactions to propel their loads into space. Many machines rely on gravity, falling bodies, springs, and all of Newton's laws of motion to make them work. Continue to learn about physics and you will gain a better appreciation of the machines around you. ■

FUN FACT

Charles Babbage designed the first mechanical calculator in 1832; he called it the *Difference Engine*. The machine contained nearly 2,000 levers and gears. Numbers were represented by the teeth on the gears. A handle was turned to drive the gears in the first column which in turn moved other gears to allow the user to add numbers mechanically. Modern calculators are mostly electronic, but Babbage's machine made the development of modern calculators possible.

Replica of a portion of Babbage's machine

MACHINE IDENTIFICATION

Complete the "Machine Identification" worksheet by identifying as many simple machines inside the complex machines shown.

WHAT DID WE LEARN?

• What are all modern machines comprised of?

• Name several machines in your home.

TAKING IT FURTHER

• How would your life be different if you had no modern machines?

INTERNAL COMBUSTION ENGINE

To the right is a diagram of an internal combustion engine. Explain how each part uses Newton's laws of motion to make the automobile move. Also explain the mechanical advantage of simple machines used to make the engine work and to make the automobile move.

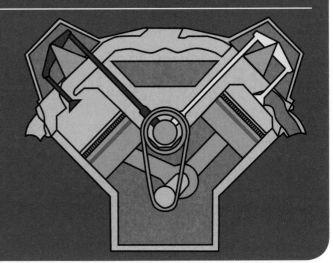

Use of Machines

Using Simple Machines: Final Project

Putting it all together

LESSON
34

Build your own machine.

We have covered a lot of ground in this book. We have learned about potential and kinetic energy. We have learned about forces, inertia, and momentum. These terms help us describe the motion of all objects.

We have examined many simple machines including inclined planes, levers, wheels, gears, and pulleys. These machines are the basis of all modern machines.

Speed, acceleration, and velocity help us describe how objects are moving, and Newton's laws of motion help us understand why objects move the way they do.

You have seen how God used periodic and circular motion when He set the universe in place. You have seen how many scientists have observed and tested the laws God put into place and have used that knowledge to create modern machines. ■

FINAL PROJECT: BUILD A MACHINE

Obviously, man does not have the same creative powers that God does. But the Bible tells us that man was created in God's image. People have creativity because God has creativity. Use some of your creativity to design your own machine. It can be as simple or complex as you like, but it must do something and you must be able to explain the physical principles behind what it does.

If you need some ideas to help you get started, consider designing one of the following:

- A better mouse trap
- A toy that is powered by a spring or rubber band
- A device to help out in the kitchen (for chopping, slicing, spreading, etc.)
- A device to help you clean your teeth better

Draw a diagram of your design. Label all the parts. Then write an explanation of how your device works. If you have the parts necessary to build your device, build it and try it out.

WHAT DID WE LEARN?

- What are Newton's three laws of motion?
- What is the difference between speed and velocity?
- What is the first law of thermodynamics?
- What is the law of conservation of momentum?

TAKING IT FURTHER

- What is your favorite machine? How does it demonstrate the laws listed here?

SCIENTIST RESEARCH

Choose a famous physicist and write a report on him. Below are some names to choose from. If you choose one of the people covered in a special feature in this book, you should do additional research to learn more about that scientist.

- Sir Isaac Newton
- Nicolaus Copernicus
- Galileo Galilei
- Leonardo da Vinci
- Albert Einstein
- Aristotle
- Archimedes
- Edmond Halley
- Henry Cavendish
- Johannes Kepler

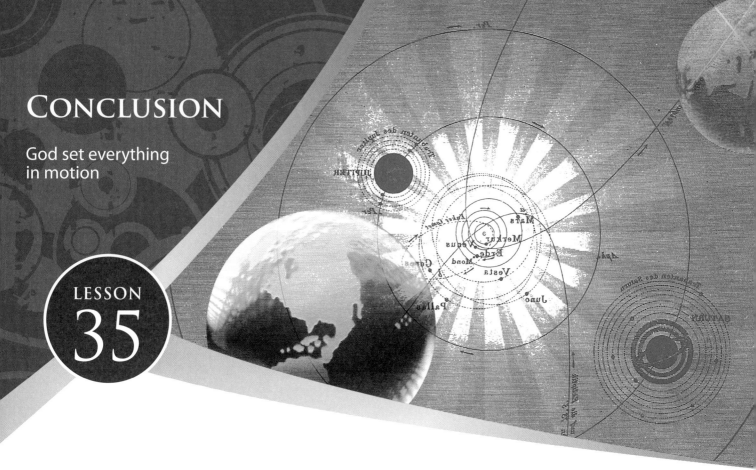

CONCLUSION

God set everything in motion

God designed the universe.

We have talked a lot about Galileo and Isaac Newton and the discoveries they made. These remarkable men are credited with some of the most important scientific discoveries of the modern age. In particular, Isaac Newton is credited with defining many of the laws of physics that help us design our modern machines. However, men did not invent any of the laws of physics. God designed the universe and set the laws by which it operates. When you think about this, it is absolutely amazing the way God designed the universe. God created gravity. God set the stars and planets in place. God made friction. God did it all!

Take time to consider how awesome God is. Read Psalm 19:1–6. Think about how the heavens declare God's glory. This passage tells us that even though the universe does not have a physical voice, it shows God's glory every day by the movement of the sun, moon, and stars. Hundreds of years before Galileo and Newton, people understood that the heavenly bodies moved in circular paths and they knew this demonstrated God's mighty power. Now read Psalm 19:7–14. If God is awesome enough to make the physical laws, then He is awesome enough that we must consider and follow His spiritual laws. Please pray the words of Psalm 19:14: "Let the words of my mouth and the meditation of my heart be acceptable in Your sight, O LORD, my strength and my Redeemer." ■

Glossary

Acceleration   Rate at which an object's velocity is increasing

Angular momentum   Momentum of an object moving through a circle

Ballistics   The study of objects moving through the air

Bevel gear   Gear system that can connect non-parallel gear shafts

Block and tackle   A pulley system with one fixed and one or more moveable pulleys

Bolt   Screw with a flat tip

Buoyancy   Force exerted by liquids and gases equal to mass of displaced fluid

Center of mass/Center of gravity   Point where the mass of an object appears to be concentrated

Centripetal force   Force applied to an object that causes it to move in a circle

Deceleration/Negative acceleration   Rate at which an object's velocity is decreasing

Distance principle   In order to use less force you must apply the force over a longer distance

Dynamics   Study of why things move the way they do

Efficiency   Amount of energy the machine puts out compared to the amount of energy put into the machine

Effort arm   The solid bar of a lever

Effort   Force applied to move the resistance

Energy   The ability to perform work

First law of motion/Law of inertia   An object at rest will remain at rest and an object in motion will remain in motion unless acted upon by an outside force

First law of thermodynamics   In a closed system, energy can neither be created nor destroyed, only transformed or transferred

First-class lever   Fulcrum is between the effort and the resistance

Force   A push or a pull

Frame of reference   Point of view from which movement is being observed

Friction   Force that resists movement

Fulcrum   Point around which the effort arm rotates

Gear   Special wheel with teeth

Inclined plane   Ramp

Inertia   An object's tendency to stay in the position it is in

Kinematics   The study of how things move

Kinetic energy   Energy that is being used

Law of conservation of energy   Energy cannot be created or destroyed, it can only change forms

Law of conservation of mass   Matter cannot be created or destroyed, it can only change forms

Law of conservation of momentum   Changes of momentum in a closed system must be equal

Law of gravitation   Any two bodies attract each other with a force proportional to the product of their masses and inversely proportional to the square of the distance between them

Law of moments   The farther the effort is from the fulcrum compared to the distance the resistance is from the fulcrum, the less effort that is required to move the resistance; $W_1D_1 = W_2D_2$ where W is weight and D is distance

Lever   Solid bar that rotates around a fixed point

Lubricant   Substance that reduces friction

Mechanical advantage   Ability to move an object using less force

Mechanical energy   Energy of motion

Mechanics   Study of motion

Momentum   Movement due to mass and velocity in a particular direction

Net force   Sum of all the forces exerted on an object

Oscillation   Movement between two extremes

Pendulum   A string or bar with a weight at the end that is free to swing back and forth

Periodic motion   Movement that repeats at a regular interval

Pitch   Distance between the threads of a screw or bolt

Potential energy   Energy that is being stored

Power   Rate at which work is done

Rack and pinion   Gear system that changes rotational motion to linear motion

Relative motion   motion of one object with respect to another

Resistance   Weight that is moved by the lever

Screw   Inclined plane wrapped around a cylinder or cone

Second law of motion/Law of acceleration   The force required to move an object is equal to the object's mass times its acceleration

Second-class lever   Resistance is between the effort and the fulcrum

Speed   Rate at which an object changes position; distance covered in a period of time

Spur gear   Gear system that can connect parallel gear shafts

Tensile strength   The amount of tension a material can withstand

Tension   A continuous pull on an object

Terminal velocity   Maximum speed of a falling body

Third law of motion/Law of action and reaction   For every action there is an equal and opposite reaction

Third-class lever   Effort is between the resistance and the fulcrum

Velocity   Speed and direction that an object is moving

Wedge   Two inclined planes placed bottom to bottom

Work   Change in position due to an applied force (force times distance)

Worm gear   Gear system where the wheel turns a threaded shaft

CHALLENGE GLOSSARY

Amplitude Amount an object moves in each direction around the mean position

Centrifugal force Imaginary or apparent force that is equal and opposite to the centripetal force that keeps an object moving in a circle.

Cycle One complete movement or revolution

Damping the process causing the oscillations to die down

Frequency Number of cycles in one second

Hooke's law A spring stretches or compresses proportional to the force applied

Magnitude Length of the vector arrow

Mean position Position about which the oscillation occurs

Period Time for one complete cycle

Physical law Laws put in place by God to govern how things work in the universe

Vector An arrow representing an object's speed and direction

INDEX

angular momentum   90, 91–93, 118
Archimedes   4, 22, 34–35, 42, 44, 116
Babbage, Charles   113
Bacon, Sir Francis   84
Bassler, Johann Ernst   19
block and tackle   54–55, 118
buoyancy   21–23, 35, 118
capstan   50
center of mass   5, 71, 87–89, 118
centrifugal force   91, 93, 120
centrifuge   93
centripetal force   91–93, 95, 118, 120
circular motion   5, 8, 90–92, 99, 115
conservation of energy   4, 7, 13–14, 118
cycle   99, 101, 120
Leonardo da Vinci   19, 116
damping   99, 101, 120
deceleration   63–64, 118
dynamics   5, 71–72, 118
effort arm   41–45, 48, 118
Einstein, Albert   5, 14, 66–70, 116
first law of motion   5, 71–74, 118
first law of thermodynamics   13–14, 116, 118
Foucault, Leon   101
frame of reference   58–59, 64, 66–68, 72, 118
frequency   99, 101, 120
fulcrum   41–49, 54, 107, 109–110, 118–119
Galileo   72, 74, 81, 84–85, 95, 98, 102–104, 116–117

gear   4, 31, 33, 49, 51–53, 55, 103, 113, 115, 118–119
gravity   5, 8–10, 12, 21–23, 64, 68, 71, 73–74, 78, 80–83, 85–89, 91, 94–96, 99–100, 103, 113, 117–118
Great Pyramid   106
gyroscope   68, 92
Halley, Edmond   94–95, 116
Hooke's law   21, 23, 120
Huygens, Christian   5, 103–104
inclined plane   33, 36–38, 40, 118–119
Joule, James   15
Kepler, Johannes   5, 95, 97–98, 116
kinematics   5, 57–59, 118
kinetic energy   4, 7, 10–13, 101, 115, 118
law of conservation of energy   13–14, 118
law of conservation of momentum   16–17, 116, 118
law of moments   41, 43–44, 119
law of universal gravitation   80–83, 86, 94–96, 119
lever   4, 31, 33, 35, 41–48, 50–52, 54–55, 107, 109–110, 113, 115, 118–119
mean position   99, 101, 120
mechanics   8–9, 119
Michelson, Albert   68
Morley, Edward   68
Newton, Sir Isaac   23, 32, 34, 72, 80, 94, 116–117
Newton's laws of motion   72, 91, 96, 113–115
oscillation   99, 101, 119–120

pendulum   5, 11, 90, 99–104, 113, 119
potential energy   7, 10–13, 99, 101, 119
pulley   4, 31, 33, 35, 54–56, 113, 115, 118
rack and pinion   51–53, 119
Scott, David R   82
screw   4, 20, 31, 33–35, 38–40, 55, 118–119
second law of motion   5, 71, 75–77, 119
Stonehenge   32, 106–108
tensile strength   21–23, 119
tension   21–23, 74, 119

theory of relativity   5, 57, 66–70
third law of motion   5, 71, 78–79, 92, 119
wedge   4, 31, 38–40, 55, 110–111, 113, 119
wheel and axle   20, 48–50